Life in
Ancient Greece

Other titles in the *Living History* series include:

Life in Ancient Greece

Don Nardo

San Diego, CA

© 2016 ReferencePoint Press, Inc.
Printed in the United States

For more information, contact:
ReferencePoint Press, Inc.
PO Box 27779
San Diego, CA 92198
www.ReferencePointPress.com

LIBRARY OF CONGRESS CATALOGING-IN-PUBLICATION DATA

Nardo, Don, 1947–
    Life in ancient Greece / by Don Nardo.
        pages cm. -- (Living history)
    Includes bibliographical references and index.
    ISBN 978-1-60152-804-9 (hardback) -- ISBN 1-60152-804-3 (hardback)
 1. Greece--Civilization--To 146 B.C. 2. Greece--Social life and customs. I. Title.
    DF78.N373   2016
    938--dc23
                                                                    2014040439

Contents

Foreword

Hist ory is a complex and multifaceted discipline that embraces many different areas of human activity. Given the expansive possibilities for the study of history, it is significant that since the advent of formal writing in the Ancient Near East over six thousand years ago, the contents of most nonfiction historical literature have been overwhelmingly limited to politics, religion, warfare, and diplomacy.

Beginning in the 1960s, however, the focus of many historical works experienced a substantive change worldwide. This change resulted from the efforts and influence of an ever-increasing number of progressive contemporary historians who were entering the halls of academia. This new breed of academician, soon accompanied by many popular writers, argued for a major revision of the study of history, one in which the past would be presented from the ground up. What this meant was that the needs, wants, and thinking of ordinary people should and would become an integral part of the human record. As British historian Mary Fulbrook wrote in her 2005 book, *The People's State: East German Society from Hitler to Honecker,* students should be able to view "history with the people put back in." This approach to understanding the lives and times of people of the past has come to be known as social history. According to contemporary social historians, national and international affairs should be viewed not only from the perspective of those empowered to create policy but also through the eyes of those over whom power is exercised.

The American historian and best-selling author, Louis "Studs" Terkel, was one of the pioneers in the field of social history. He is best remembered for his oral histories, which were firsthand accounts of everyday life drawn from the recollections of interviewees who lived during pivotal events or periods in history. Terkel's first book, *Division Street America* (published in 1967), focuses on urban living in and around Chicago and is a compilation of seventy interviews of immigrants and native-born Americans. It was followed by several other oral histories including *Hard Times* (the 1930s depression), *Working* (people's feelings about their jobs), and his 1985 Pulitzer Prize–winning *The Good War* (about life in America before, during, and after World War II).

In keeping with contemporary efforts to present history by people and about people, ReferencePoint's *Living History* series offers students a journey through recorded history as recounted by those who lived it. While modern sources such as those found in *The Good War* and on radio and TV interviews are readily available, those dating to earlier periods in history are scarcer and often more obscure the further back in time one investigates. These important primary sources are there nonetheless waiting to be discovered in literary formats such as posters, letters, and diaries, and in artifacts such as vases, coins, and tombstones. And they are also found in places as varied as ancient Mesopotamia, Charles Dickens's England, and Nazi concentration camps. The *Living History* series uncovers these and other available sources as they relate the "living history" of real people to their student readers.

Important Events

ca. 776
The traditional date for the first Olympic Games, held at Olympia in southwestern Greece.

480–479
The Persian king Xerxes leads a huge invasion force into Greece, and in a series of epic battles the Greeks expel the invaders.

490
A small Athenian force utterly defeats an army of invading Persians on the plain of Marathon.

594
The Athenian statesman Solon negotiates a political settlement that gives a significant amount of authority to commoners.

508
Athens introduces the world's first democracy.

BCE 800   750   700 ••• 600   550   500

ca. 735–715
Sparta conquers its neighbor, Messenia, and brutally enslaves its citizenry.

534
The Athenians introduce a new public festival, the City Dionysia, featuring humanity's first known formal theatrical presentations.

464
Sparta suffers heavy damage in an earthquake, and its slaves, the *helots*, rebel. Eventually, the insurrection is crushed.

ca. 500–323
The years of Greece's Classical Age, as determined by modern scholars.

of Ancient Greece

461
In Athens a leading democratic politician named Pericles becomes the city's most influential leader.

404
Athens surrenders, ending the Peloponnesian War.

438
The Athenians dedicate the completed Parthenon temple to their patron goddess, Athena.

399
The Athenian philosopher Socrates is falsely accused of corrupting the city's youth, tried, found guilty, and sentenced to death.

431
Sparta declares war on Athens, commencing the ruinous Peloponnesian War.

450	425	400	375	350

447
Construction begins on a major new temple complex atop Athens's Acropolis, including two temples—the Erechtheum and Parthenon—dedicated to the goddess Athena.

423
The Athenian comic playwright Aristophanes writes *Clouds*, in which he lampoons the philosopher Socrates.

430–429
A deadly plague strikes Athens and kills many people, including Pericles.

371
The city-state of Thebes decisively defeats the widely feared Spartan army, and the long-enslaved Messenians regain their freedom.

Introduction

An Extraordinary Legacy

Modern Greece is a small country of humble means and influence. Moreover, in recent years it has undergone a number of serious economic problems, at times hovering near the brink of bankruptcy. One of the main reasons it has managed to stay solvent and afloat is that it enjoys one of the strongest tourist industries in the world.

Unlike Most That Had Gone Before

The reasons so many people from around the globe travel to Greece each year are historical and cultural. Long ago, that now modest little land was the central focus of one of the grandest, most influential societies in human history. In fact, most modern historians feel that the Greeks largely invented Western, or European-based, civilization. This was because life in Greece was based on a compelling set of cultural attributes unlike most that had gone before. First among these were the Greeks' highly distinctive arts, architecture, literature, political concepts, social and military customs, and philosophic and scientific ideas. Second, they possessed a unique combination of creativity and optimism about life. They also displayed an extraordinary competitive drive and sheer audacity in promoting their customs, ideas, and interests.

> **WORDS IN CONTEXT**
> **audacity**
> An unusual sense of confidence and daring.

Thanks to these unique qualities, the Greeks stood at the forefront of Western civilization for almost two thousand years. When the Greek lands were conquered and politically absorbed by the Romans in the second and first centuries BCE, the conquerors did not destroy Greek civilization. The Romans, who were great cultural copiers, were strongly impressed, even awed, by Greek culture. Indeed, they absorbed so much of it that they themselves changed as a people. In short order, a new civilization—the so-called Greco-Roman—emerged.

The result was that when the western Roman Empire disintegrated in the fifth and sixth centuries CE, the profound cultural legacy it passed on to medieval Europe contained much of what made life in Greece so brilliant and exceptional. Thereby, the Greeks' extraordinary legacy survived in diverse ways. It also eventually passed on to early modern Europe and the distant lands Europeans colonized, including the United States. This is why so many elements of Greek life and culture exist in the very fabric of modern Western society.

Many Greek Cultural Survivals

Some of these elements of ancient Greek life are clearly observable as Greek in origin and celebrated as such. Every four years, for instance, most of the world's nations take part in the Olympic Games. Based directly on the original version, held at Olympia in southwestern Greece, the modern version still features several of the same events that everyday ancient Greeks trained for and competed in. Another clearly recognizable element of Greek life that lives on is architectural in nature. Thousands of today's government buildings, banks, and college buildings are graced by stately rows of columns topped by elegant triangular gables, sometimes filled with carved statues. These are among the major facets of classical Greek temple architecture.

In contrast, numerous other elements of ancient Greek life are so delicately entwined within modern life that most people are unaware of their Greek origins. Greek theater is a perfect and potent example. The concept of actors reciting scripted lines before an audience was invented in Athens in the sixth century BCE. Over time, the theater institution became elaborate, highly varied, and spread to other lands and peoples. Today's plays, television programs, and movies are all latter-day

Theatergoers in ancient Greece await the start of a play. The concept of actors reciting scripted lines before an audience developed first in Athens and then spread to other lands, as did many other aspects of Greek culture.

adaptations of the Athenian originals. (The Athenians even introduced the concept of the theater ticket.)

Among the nearly countless other examples of surviving Greek culture are public gyms, of which the Greeks had at least one in every town; wrestling and boxing events; enlightened political systems and customs, including democracy, town hall meetings, and legislative bills and speeches; going to court to sue for personal grievances and justice; publishing and reading essays, novels, biographies, and literary critiques;

attending universities to pursue higher learning; studying and debating philosophical ideas; and pondering the nature of the universe (which the Greeks called the cosmos) and other scientific concepts. All of these things exist now because they were a part of ancient Greek life.

Profound and Noble Concepts

Certain central aspects of Western thinking about human nature and fundamental civil rights also originated in ancient Greek life. Among the noblest and most profound of these concepts is the conviction that each person possesses inherent dignity and worth. At the very heart of Greek thought, the late, great classical scholar C.M. Bowra wrote, was "an unshakable belief in the worth of the individual man." In past ages, when most regions of the planet were dominated by kings and other absolute monarchs, he explained, "the Greeks were evolving their belief that a man must be respected not as an instrument of an omnipotent overlord, but for his own sake." Furthermore, "Nature nursed the Greeks in a hard school, but this made them conscious of themselves and their worth. Without this self-awareness, they would never have made their most important contribution to human experience: the belief that a man must be honored for his individual worth and treated with respect just because he is himself."[1]

> **WORDS IN CONTEXT**
> **enlightened**
> Displaying progressive, tolerant, open-minded ideas and beliefs, especially democratic ones.

Thus, what the Greeks thought about themselves and how they incorporated such ideas into their everyday lives still shapes what many people think and do today. Their politics, customs, beliefs, inventions, and special outlook on the human condition have affected the course of Western civilization more than those of any other single people. An important result of that fact is that in a sense, ancient Greek civilization did not die out. It still lives on, in crucial and vibrant pieces, in the supportive structure of modern Western life and institutions. As long as Western society survives, therefore, the Greeks' dynamic spirit will remain, alive and well, at its core.

Chapter One

Houses and
Their Contents

The ancient Greeks called their land Hellas (which they pronounced eh-LAH-thah) and themselves Hellenes (EL-ee-nas). For their civilization, life did not remain static and unchanged over the centuries. The situations and customs of daily life naturally changed over time. But for convenience, most modern studies of Greek life concentrate on the Classical Age. Strictly speaking, it lasted from about 500 to 300 BCE and was the fruitful era when Greek arts, literature, and democratic political reforms reached their height of development.

It is also important to recognize where the ancient Greeks lived. At first glance, it might seem perfectly obvious that they resided in Greece. But the geographical region that makes up the modern nation of Greece—the Greek mainland and several nearby islands—was only part of the Greek sphere of life and influence in ancient times. At its zenith, that sphere also covered western Anatolia (what is now Turkey), much of the island of Sicily (off the southern Italian coast), and many coastal regions scattered around the Mediterranean and Black Seas.

A Fierce and Obstinate National Spirit

Besides defining *when* and *where* ancient Greece was, it is important to know *what* it was. First, it was not a unified country, as modern Greece is. Through much of the ancient era, the Greeks lived in hundreds of separate city-states (and for a while a few larger kingdoms). They called a city-state a *polis*. On average, it was made up of a town, or urban area, often built around a central hill called an acropolis. There, the local population could more easily defend itself from attack during wartime. Surrounding a polis's urban area was a network of small supporting villages and farms.

Significantly, the far-flung *poleis* (plural of *polis*) evolved differing political systems and social customs and viewed themselves as tiny separate nations. In the words of noted scholar Alfred Zimmern, each city-state stood apart as "a complete world of its own." It had "a fierce and obstinate national spirit" that knew "no allegiance to a sovereign beyond its horizon" and saw "home rule as the very breath of its being."[2]

Finally, it cannot be assumed that the inhabitants of these separate and diverse states experienced everyday life the same way. There were different traditions, laws, and customs among many of them. A large number of similarities surely existed as well. After all, the peoples of these states all spoke Greek, worshipped the same gods, and recognized the same myths about ancient origins and heroes.

The problem for modern observers is that surviving evidence for life in the vast majority of ancient Greek states is very scarce, scattered, and incomplete. Experts have only recently started to reconstruct their histories, beliefs, customs, and habits. In stark contrast, most substantial, important, firsthand knowledge of ancient Greek civilization comes from Athens, the largest and most populous of all the city-states. So the bulk of what is known about the Greeks centers on Athenian history, writers, ideas, and customs. This means that the extent to which life in other Greek states differed from life in Athens is frequently unclear.

> **WORDS IN CONTEXT**
> **acropolis**
> "High place of the city"; in ancient Greece, a town's central hill.

One major exception is Sparta, the only other ancient Greek state about which a fair amount is known. Sparta was located roughly 150 miles (241 km) southwest of Athens, and during the Classical Age it and Athens were famously archenemies. This was largely because they were culturally very different and tended to distrust each other. With occasional exceptions, the conservative, reclusive Spartans rejected the liberal, outgoing Athenians' emphasis on creativity, the arts, literature, and democratic institutions. Instead, Sparta focused most of its energies

Ancient Greece (circa 500 BCE)

on maintaining a rigid military system that stifled the creative spirit and produced the strongest land army in the Greek sphere.

Modern historians think that Sparta was very atypical of most Greek states. The consensus, by contrast, is that a majority of poleis more or less emulated Athens. But any attempt to reconstruct ancient Greek life must at times describe Sparta to show how much some Greeks differed from the norm.

Splendor Versus Modesty

If most city-states across the classical Greek sphere were indeed culturally much like Athens, it makes sense to begin an examination of Greek life there. Moreover, the logical place in Athens to start is the most basic communal unit—the home. As a ballpark figure, the fourth-century-BCE Athenian historian Xenophon said that Athens had ten thousand houses in his day. None of these residences have survived intact. Although fairly large portions of the city's renowned temples and other public buildings *have* survived to the present, all that is left of its private homes are a few stone foundations.

Considering how huge and splendid Athens's temples were, it may be surprising to some people today that Athenian houses tended to be extremely modest in size. In fact, the vast majority of private homes, including those of the rich and powerful, were smaller than the average modern middle-class home. Even some classical Greeks felt the need to remark on this seeming oddity. One was a contemporary of Xenophon— the Athenian orator Demosthenes. The latter recalled the simplicity of the houses in which Pericles and other leading politicians of the previous century dwelled. The public buildings "which they left behind them to adorn our city—temples, harbors, and their accessories," Demosthenes stated, "were so great and so fair that we who come after must despair of ever surpassing them." Yet in comparison, he added, "the private houses of those who rose to power were so modest" that they were "not a whit more splendid than those of their [poorer] neighbors."[3]

Part of the reason for this unexpected situation was that most Greek men, who owned nearly all the houses, spent very little time in them. They preferred to busy themselves with trade, shopping, politics, athletics, and other activities. To them, therefore, the home was mainly a place to sleep and to enjoy the evening meal with the family. So such a dwelling did not need to be large and expensively furnished.

Also, in Athens and other Greek cities, the urban centers were laid out to show off the temples, marketplace (called the *agora*), theaters, and other communal gathering places. As historian R.E. Wycherley says, "the houses filled in the rest," standing along narrow streets with the "houses huddled together." This, Wycherley points out, often created crowded conditions that would be "intolerable by modern standards."[4]

The outsides of those modest-sized, crammed-together houses were mostly plain, with little in the way of decoration. They were also whitewashed to reflect sunlight and thereby keep the interiors cooler. It was in

In Their Own Words

The Practical Way to Build a House

As a young man, the fourth-century-BCE Athenian soldier and historian Xenophon was well acquainted with his countryman, the philosopher and social critic Socrates. Years later Xenophon penned a book (the *Memorabilia*) containing recollections of his friend and the gems of practical wisdom he had often displayed. In this excerpt, Socrates advises that in building a house a person should be practical and take advantage of natural forces, including the sun and its rays. "Socrates seemed to me," Xenophon wrote,

> to be teaching the principle that buildings should satisfy practical requirements. He approached the question in this sort of way: "If a man is to have the sort of house he needs, ought he to contrive to make it as pleasant and convenient as possible to live in?" When I admitted this, he said: "Isn't it pleasant to have a house which is cool in summer and warm in winter?" When I agreed to this too, he said: "Well, in houses that have a south [facing] aspect, in winter the sun shines into the [courtyard], while in summer it passes over our heads and over the roof and casts a shade. So, if this is the desired effect, one should build the south side higher so as not to shut off the winter sun, and the north side lower so as to avoid exposure to cold winds."

Xenophon, "Memorabilia," in Xenophon, *Conversations of Socrates*, trans. Hugh Tredennick and Robin Waterfield. New York: Penguin, 1990, pp. 159–60.

these interiors, with their distinctive layout and contents, that the most personal aspects of everyday life took place.

Country Versus City

The type of layout and furnishings of Greek homes depended to some degree on where they were located. The words of Xenophon and Wycherley focus on urban homes, or townhouses. But a great many Greeks lived in the countryside. Agriculture was the foundation of the city-states' economies, and farming was the most widespread occupation. As a result, in a typical Greek polis the overall population of the countryside was larger than that of the urban center. According to recent studies, for example, about 60 percent of the population of Thebes, an important city-state lying north of Athens, lived in the villages and farms surrounding the central town.

As near as modern experts can tell, a rural village of that era consisted of a few modest huts clustered together for mutual security. The farmers who dwelled in the huts got up each morning and walked to their nearby fields. However, some farmers preferred to build stand-alone huts right beside their fields.

Whether a hut was located within a village or by itself, it tended to be constructed mostly of natural, mainly perishable materials. These included wood, thatch (bundled plant materials), fieldstones, sun-dried clay bricks, and so forth. Most often, such a country house had one, two, or occasionally three or four rooms. The floors were composed of hard-packed dirt, usually covered by straw mats and/or flagstones. Meanwhile, a simple stone-lined hearth located in the main room gave the family both cooking facilities and some extra warmth on chilly winter nights.

Townhouses: Materials and Layout

As one would expect, most of the farmers who lived in those country dwellings spent the majority of their time outside of the urban center. Periodically, however, a farmer filled up one or more wagons with freshly harvested crops and headed for the city's agora to sell them. Once inside the urban center, the farmer passed at least some townhouses on his way to the agora. Physically speaking, many of them resembled rural homes in some ways. Such a city residence had a stone foundation, like that of a country hut, for instance, and walls made of clay bricks. The builders sometimes added wooden timbers to reinforce the bricks. Yet the walls were neither strong nor durable, because the clay started crumbling after only a few years, which led to the need for repeated repairs.

In addition, thieves had little problem burrowing through those fragile walls. This sad fact of life in the urban areas led Demosthenes to chide his fellow Athenians, saying they "should not be surprised at the number of thefts that are committed." What else should they expect when "we have thieves of brass [boldness], while the walls of our houses are only made of clay?"[5]

The reason that most thieves did not crawl through the windows of these homes is that windows were few in number and most often located well above street level. The front doors situated on the ground level almost always opened outward. So exiting one's home could create a danger to passersby, who might suffer a nasty knock on the forehead if a door suddenly opened in front of them. Two precautions were generally taken to keep this from happening. First, builders made front doors unusually narrow; second, it became customary for a person leaving the house to vigorously knock on the door's inside as a warning to people in the street.

One difference between country houses and urban homes was that townhouses were often larger and had a wide variety of layouts. Many had rooms that surrounded and opened into a small central courtyard that was open to the sky and weather. Others featured rooms that opened into a long central hallway called a *pastas*. Whether there was a courtyard or *pastas*, the poorest homes had two or three small rooms, whereas average residences had four to seven mostly tiny rooms and now and then a few more.

Bedchambers, Kitchens, and Other Rooms

Still another variation in the layout of townhouses was that some featured only a ground floor, whereas others had two levels. The upstairs

An early modern painting depicts the country house of a well-to-do ancient Greek farmer. His field hands and slaves are gathering to celebrate a seasonal agricultural festival.

space was most often divided into several very small cubicles, generally bedchambers. Each was just big enough to fit a single bed and a wooden chest for storing personal items. (Closets had not yet been invented.)

Sometimes one or two of these little rooms, and/or a bit of cramped attic space, housed the family's slaves.

The ground-floor rooms were usually larger and served fairly standard functions that rarely varied from house to house. It was common, for instance, for a townhouse to have an *exedra*, a sitting area with one or two sides open to the inner courtyard. There was also a kitchen. To cook food, people employed either braziers, metal containers that burned wood or charcoal, or a stone-lined hearth similar to the ones in country houses. Studies of house foundations in northern Greece suggest that some homes had storage bins for fruit, bread, and kitchenware.

The smallest houses, including rural ones, did not have bathrooms. Instead, a person used a chamber pot that he or she emptied by hand into a ditch, cesspool (underground pit), or sewer outside. (The Athenians employed cesspools in the fifth century BCE, but constructed public sewers in the century that followed.)

A number of larger townhouses did have bathrooms, which were tiny by today's standards. In some the toilet was basically a latrine—a seat resting atop a pit that collected the wastes. But modern excavators have found that some houses did have modern-shaped toilets fashioned of terra-cotta (baked clay). One discovered at Olynthus, a polis in northern Greece, was equipped with terra-cotta channels that carried wastes to the town's sewers. Some bathrooms had tubs, also made of terra-cotta, for bathing. Most often, a person or his or her slave used buckets to fill the tub, and afterward the dirty water drained to the outside through a terra-cotta channel at floor level.

Other common rooms in Greek townhouses included a small dining room close by the kitchen; the *andron*, an area used exclusively by the male head of the household to dine and entertain his adult friends; and sometimes one or more specialized workrooms, usually in homes owned by artisans of various types. In and around Athens's ancient Agora, for example, archaeologists have found the remnants of houses belonging to potters who created their wares in their home workrooms.

WORDS IN CONTEXT

exedra

A sitting area, often having one or two sides open to the inner courtyard.

Furnishings, Light, and Heat

Those workrooms were cluttered with workbenches, stools, tools of various kinds, and, of course, the raw materials the artisan used in his or her trade. In contrast, the furniture and decorations of a majority of Greek homes were on the sparse side compared with the average modern house. Most walls, for example, were covered by a simple, plain coat of plaster. A minority of well-to-do homeowners were able to afford handsome wall decorations. Most often these consisted of frescoes (paintings done on wet plaster) and/or hanging tapestries made of embroidered cloth. A few more affluent families also had the money to commission murals or designs made of mosaic tiles in some rooms.

As for furniture, most was fairly plain and constructed with everyday use in mind rather than for its decorative qualities. Couches and beds consisted of simple wooden frames covered in thin padding stuffed with feathers or animal fur. Throw pillows provided some extra comfort. Bedspreads were handwoven on looms and in some cases dyed in bright colors.

Square- and oval-shaped tables, along with stools, chairs, and benches, were normally constructed of wood and uncomplicated in design. The storage chests found in many rooms of an average home were also made of wood. One important difference between these and modern interior rooms was that the ancient ones rarely featured wooden doors that could be closed and locked. Rather, more often than not the Greeks hung cloth curtains in their interior doorways.

The same rooms needed some form of light after the sun went down. Most commonly, the residents employed oil lamps, small, shallow containers that burned wicks floating in olive oil. Candles were also used for interior lighting. Heat was sometimes also a household need. As long as the air was only cool, as opposed to uncomfortably cold, most Greeks simply huddled with a spouse, sibling, or friend beneath several layers of bedding. To provide warmth on the coldest nights, the braziers used for cooking gave off some heat. A plus was that they could usually be moved easily from room to room. If that approach was not sufficient to overcome the chill, one could grab a bedspread and sleep beside the main hearth.

Looking Back

Making Olive Oil

The olive oil for which the Greeks had so many uses had to be extracted from the olives in the most efficient, least wasteful manner possible. The first step in the process they developed was to crush the olives. At first, they did this by grinding them in a bowl using a mortar and pestle. Later, people began using a large stone saucer. According to classical scholars Lesley and Roy A. Adkins, it had "a central pillar, which supported the pivot for one or two millstones that could be rolled around the saucer to crush the olives." After the olives were crushed, they were pressed to extract the oil. This could be done by various means, such as placing a heavy weight on bags or baskets of olives. A simple mechanical press was also used, consisting of a large wooden beam that was anchored at one end and acted as a lever. Crushed olives were placed in a permeable container (possibly of cloth) on a hard surface beneath the lever, and the other end of the lever was forced downward to squash the container and its contents. This was done by ropes and levers, a lever, or a screw mechanism in Hellenistic times [the period directly following the Classical period]. The pressing was usually done on a wooden or stone pressing bed, with a channel and spout to collect the oil. Olive oil was used for various purposes, including food, lighting fuel, medicines, and skin oils.

Lesley Adkins and Roy A. Adkins, *Handbook to Life in Ancient Greece*. New York: Facts On File, 2005, p. 175.

Meals and Food Items

Next to sleeping, the most frequent activities performed inside the house were preparing and eating the daily meals. In the Classical period, most people did not eat breakfast. Instead, they had a light lunch, called *ariston*, and in the evening they enjoyed their main meal, *deipnon*. Toward the end of that era, breakfast, or *akratisma*, was adopted in the Greek lands and remained customary in the centuries that followed. Family members usually ate their meals together, except when the head of the household entertained his guests in the *andron*. In that case the women and children of the house ate in the regular dining room or elsewhere on the premises.

Once breakfast became common, it was the smallest meal of the day. Most people had a bit of bread (at times soaked in wine), plus a piece of fruit and/or a slice of cheese. Roughly the same kinds of foods were eaten at lunch, though in somewhat larger quantities. For the main meal, the Greeks had bread once again, but added to it vegetables, soup, and fish, along with dessert, consisting of items such as nuts, cake, and fruit.

Meat from goats, sheep, or pigs was occasionally eaten at supper. Also popular across the Greek sphere were birds, including ducks, geese, owls, pigeons, cranes, swans, and several others. Yet fish provided by far the bulk of the flesh foods eaten. Most of the larger Greek towns were situated on or near seashores, so fish of various types were accessible to most people at reasonable cost.

> **WORDS IN CONTEXT**
> *ariston*
> A light lunch eaten in the ancient Greek lands.

Meanwhile, the reliance on bread at all three meals demonstrates that grains such as barley and wheat were important staple foods. Wheat grew in some parts of the Greek mainland, but in general the climate and other factors made it less plentiful there. So in Classical times Athens and other big mainland city-states imported much of their wheat from foreign ports. The biggest suppliers of that grain were Greek cities that ringed the Black Sea's coasts.

Vegetables and fruits were also common staples for Greek diners. Among their favorite vegetables were onions, mushrooms, lentils, cabbage, beets, garlic, lettuce, basil, cucumbers, mustard greens, and rad-

Olives are harvested and pressed for use as cooking oil, as fuel for lamps, and as a base for perfumes. Olives once grew wild on the Greek mainland and nearby islands but were later cultivated by the ancient Greeks.

ishes. The most common fruits consumed were grapes, olives, apples, figs, pears, plums, pomegranates, watermelons, and sour cherries. Greek cheese was made chiefly from goat's milk, and honey was the primary sweetener in ancient Greek cooking and baking.

Two Crucial Liquids

Although grapes were widely eaten, they were also the source of one of two crucial liquids used in ancient Greek society. Grapes produced wine, which was without question the favorite drink throughout the Greek cultural sphere. The other key liquid was olive oil. It was used as a cooking medium in countless food dishes, as well as fuel for oil lamps and a base for perfumes.

Both grapes and olives grew wild on the Greek mainland and nearby islands when people first settled those regions many centuries earlier.

Over time, cultivation of these two foods became intensive, organized, and efficient. As a result, they proved essential to people's lives. According to Andrew Dalby, an expert on ancient Greek cooking, both liquids "provided cooking media and flavorings, the olive with its oil [and] the grape with its juice, both unfermented and fermented into wine."[6]

When used for drinking rather than as a cooking medium, wine was regularly mixed with water in a ratio of about two parts water to one part wine. This diluting process took place in a *krater*, a pottery bowl made specifically for that purpose. It was also customary to drink chilled wine when possible. The most common cooling method was to store the wine underground, but those who could afford it had slaves lug in containers of ice from the nearest mountains.

Because Greek wine was most often considerably watered down, it rarely made people drunk. However, on occasion some people did drink it undiluted, so drunkenness was far from unknown. It is likely that because most people were not used to the effects of full-strength wine, when they did try it they became intoxicated faster than a modern moderate wine drinker would. Moreover, an ancient Greek who binged on undiluted wine had a much higher chance of dying of alcohol poisoning than a modern binge drinker does.

> **WORDS IN CONTEXT**
> *krater*
> A pottery bowl made specifically for mixing wine and water.

The Greeks did not understand the medical reasons for such effects. So they sometimes fell back on myths and superstition to explain them. In particular, they came to see the god of vines and wine, Dionysus, as having two sides, one positive and the other negative. As one modern historian says, "Not only is he a god of life, wine, and festivities, he is also a god of destruction. Wine itself had ambiguous [uncertain] qualities. It creates good feelings, but it can also release violent, destructive passions."[7] Most Greeks in this period were very religiously devout, and this is only one of many examples of how their faith touched directly on aspects of their daily life.

Chapter Two

Family Members, Roles, and Duties

The physical layout of ancient Greek houses, along with the furniture, cooking facilities, and the meals eaten daily, naturally served the needs of the family units that occupied those dwellings. The Greeks called the family the *oikos* (EE-kos). By tradition, the chief male present—usually the husband and/or father—was the head of the family. He made the rules and in most cases enforced them, arranged for his children's education, gave money to family members who needed it, and bought or sold slaves when conditions within the household required it.

This man's wife, children, live-in relatives, if any, and slaves usually fulfilled their own traditional family roles. They obeyed his rules and did their chores and other duties, hoping to make the household run smoothly. In these ways, the fourth-century-BCE Athenian scholar and thinker Plato said, a family could sometimes be like a smaller version of a polis. "A large household may be compared to a small state,"[8] he wrote.

A Sort of Dual Status

Although men were traditionally the heads of families, they were usually not petty tyrants. Most Greek heads of households spent little time at home and delegated much of their authority to their wives or other family members. In fact, in most cases the wife and/or mother of a family actually ran the household on a day-to-day basis. In Xenophon's treatise *Oeconomicus*, an estate owner named Ischomachus states, "My wife is quite capable of looking after the house by herself!"[9]

The fact that from a practical standpoint a Greek home was run by a woman contrasted sharply with the political status of most Greek females in that era. The vast majority of women in the Greek states were second-class citizens who could neither vote nor run for public office. Moreover, except for a few women who worked outside the home, most female citizens were expected to be accompanied by a male family member (or male slave) when in public.

While inside her home, however, a woman's status and authority were significant, and more often than not she was more of a partner than a servant to her husband. Xenophon's Ischomachus informs his wife, "It seems to me, dear, that the gods with great discernment have coupled together male and female," mainly so that "they may form a perfect partnership in mutual service." Ischomachus gives several reasons for this state of affairs. One is: "Since both the indoor and the outdoor tasks demand labor and attention, God from the first adapted the woman's nature, I think, to the indoor and man's to the outdoor tasks and cares," and "we must endeavor, each of us, to do the duties allotted to us as well as possible."[10] Considering Greek women's position in public as compared to their homes, therefore, most possessed a sort of dual social status.

Preparing for Marriage

A woman's power within the home did not extend to her ability to choose a mate, however. Most Greek marriages were arranged, either by fathers or clan leaders, and it was fairly common for a young bride and groom to hardly know each other before their wedding night. The idea of falling in love did not usually enter into the picture. Assorted evidence indicates that romantic love, as people today view it, *did* exist. But it is likely that very few ancient Greek couples were lucky enough to experience it.

> **WORDS IN CONTEXT**
> *kyrios*
> In ancient Greek society, a woman's legal guardian.

What most experienced instead was a social and legal pact entered into by two men. One was the prospective bride's father, who was her legal guardian, or *kyrios*. The other was her husband-to-be, who would become her *kyrios* when they were married.

A newly married couple is conveyed to their home in an ox-drawn cart. Members of the wedding procession follow on foot, carrying torches and singing traditional wedding songs.

The agreement was sealed at a formal betrothal, almost always in front of witnesses, and some financial assets changed hands along with the bride. The most important was her dowry. It consisted of money and/or valuables her father gave her husband to aid in maintaining her in the marriage. According to noted scholar Sarah B. Pomeroy,

> The groom could use the principle [original sum], but was required to maintain his wife from the income of [the interest generated by] her dowry, computed at 18 percent annually. Upon divorce, the husband was required to return the dowry to his ex-wife's guardian, or pay interest at 18 percent. Thus, her support would often continue to be provided for, and, with her dowry intact, she would be eligible for remarriage.[11]

The Wedding

Once the parties to the marriage arrangement and dowry had agreed to the deal, it was time for the wedding celebration. No comprehensive accounts of the ceremony itself—as enacted in Athens and most other city-states—have survived. But a few historians have pieced together a credible general scenario, among them the late French scholar Robert

Flaceliere. "On the day of the wedding," he wrote, "the houses of both the bride and groom were decorated with garlands made from olive and laurel leaves, and there was a sacrifice and banquet at the house of the bride's father. The bride herself was present at this feast, veiled and wearing her finest clothes."[12]

Later that evening, Flaceliere goes on, the guests formed a procession, or formal column of marchers, to "convey the bride to her new home." She and the groom rode in "a wagon drawn by mules or oxen, with a friend of the bridegroom's to drive it." Everyone else followed on foot, carrying torches and singing a traditional wedding hymn. "When they reached the door of the groom's house, nuts and dried figs were showered on the bride," and then "the couple proceeded straight to the bridal chamber." When the door to that room had closed, the guests "sang some nuptial hymn at the tops of their voices to scare away evil spirits."[13]

In Sparta, by contrast, where social customs were frequently quite different from elsewhere, no public wedding ceremony is known to have been held. Evidence suggests that some Spartan marriages may have been arranged. But if so, it was not as formal and strict a process as in Athens. Historian Helena Schrader, an authority on ancient Sparta, explains that for Spartan women, who were not nearly as socially restricted as women in other Greek states, marriage "was never to a stranger. Spartan girls had watched, cheered, jeered, and flirted with the bachelors of the city from girlhood onward. They knew them all by name." Furthermore, if a Spartan father told his daughter he had chosen a young man for her to marry,

she would have an opinion. Nothing in Spartan law or custom prevented her from voicing it. Whether her father listened to her was another matter, but it is not likely that a Spartan man would force a husband on a daughter over his wife's opposition, and she, no less than her daughter, would know all about the eligible bachelors from watching them on the playing fields and dance floors. In short, Spartan girls might not have chosen their husbands, but they had a good chance of vetoing a truly distasteful candidate.[14]

The only surviving description of the Spartan marriage "ceremony," if it can be called that, is by the first-century-CE Greek biographer Plutarch. This strange nocturnal ritual was consistent with Sparta's highly militaristic customs, in which young men lived together in a barracks outside their homes. "The custom," Plutarch wrote, was for such a young man to capture his bride in order to seal the marriage. That bride "first shaved her head to the scalp, then dressed in a man's cloak and sandals, and laid down alone on a mattress in the dark." Meanwhile, the groom had dinner in the barracks with his male comrades. Then he would slip into the girl's room, "undo her belt, lift her, and carry her to the bed. After spending only a short time with her, he would depart discreetly so as to sleep wherever he usually did along with the other young men."[15]

Divorce Without Dishonor

Among Athenians and most other Greeks, if a couple's marriage did not work out, divorce was available without any social dishonor involved. Reasons for divorce were mostly similar to those today. Adultery was perhaps the most common one. Another example was when one spouse abused the other.

A man could get divorced simply by ordering his wife out of the house, in which case she most often returned to her father's home. It was somewhat more difficult for a woman to initiate a divorce, however. She had to convince a male relative to go to a high-ranking civic official and ask for permission on her behalf. Even if the official granted her the divorce, though, most of the time her husband got custody of the children.

Gaining Versus Losing Children

Childbirth customarily took place in the home. To announce a birth to the neighbors, parents attached an olive stem to the door if it was a boy or a bit of wool if it was a girl. After that the mother went to a local temple or shrine honoring either Artemis, a goddess who supposedly helped women through childbirth, or to the shrine of the actual deity of childbirth—Ilithyia. The woman verbally thanked the goddess and offered her a clothing item as high in quality as the family could afford.

Religious offerings were also made in a sadder circumstance—when a

Looking Back

Having a Baby

Most ancient Greek babies were born in the home and delivered by a midwife, with the help of female family members and friends. Scholar Sue Blundell, an expert on the women of ancient Greece, provides this overview of what is known about the childbirth process. In her comments she mentions a ritual bath given to mother and child immediately after the birth. Religious tradition of the time held that they were "polluted," or unclean, until they were washed.

> Women usually gave birth in a seated position, either on a birthing stool, or, in an emergency, on the lap of one of the helpers. It was probably unusual for a woman to be delivered lying down, but it was certainly not unknown. A number of Hippocratic sources [Greek medical writings] refer to the use of drugs to speed up delivery, and sometimes labor would have to be induced. One Hippocratic author describes a rather violent method whereby four female assistants seize the woman by the legs and arms and give her at least ten firm shakes, then place her on a bed with her legs in the air and subject her to more shaking by the shoulders. . . . At the moment of birth the mother's helpers uttered a ritual cry of joy, [and] once the afterbirth had been expelled, mother and child were given a ritual bath to cleanse them of the defilement of the birth process.

Sue Blundell, *Women in Ancient Greece*. Cambridge, MA: Harvard University Press, 1995, p. 111.

mother died during childbirth. It is unclear how often this occurred. But most modern experts estimate it was from 10 to 20 percent of the time, as compared to only .01 percent (one woman in 10,000) in industrialized nations today. This was partly because a majority of ancient Greek mothers were teenagers when they had their first and second children. Even today teenage mothers have a higher risk of physical problems in both pregnancy and birth. Pervasive ignorance about proper hygiene was likely another factor.

When a mother died in childbirth, her infant might or might not survive. According to Mark Golden, a leading modern scholar on the subject of ancient Greek children, from 25 to 35 percent of them died in their first year of life. In contrast, in the United States today this figure is less than 1 percent.

Greek parents were distressed by such cases of infant mortality partly for emotional reasons, of course. But there were also factors not considered particularly relevant by most people today. One was a tradition that called on parents to make sure their family line did not die out. Most people today would see this as unfortunate, but in ancient Greece it was an awful tragedy, often seen as a punishment inflicted by an angry god. Another major concern was to make certain that the community was perpetuated. The bulk of Greek city-states were small, with only a few thousand citizens. So if not enough offspring were created regularly, especially male ones, it was possible that the state might eventually lack the human resources to defend itself and thereby cease to exist.

The Importance of Adoption

An infant who survived his or her first year of life was therefore seen as a boon to both the *oikos* and to the community at large. The parents, especially the father, were particularly pleased if one of the babies they conceived was a boy. This was because the family now had a legitimate heir. A woman could inherit property and other items under certain conditions, and she could care for her elderly parents. But both tradition and community laws favored male offspring to accomplish these tasks. "In the whole range of life," Alfred Zimmern says, "there was nothing probably which the Greek man dreaded more" than to be without a male heir. There would be "no one to tend him in old age, to close his eyes in death" and to "keep alive the institutions that were so dear to him."[16]

The remedy to this situation was quite often to adopt a boy. In most cases that person was a relative, usually a nephew or cousin. This made sense, since the chief reason for taking this step was to maintain the bloodline on the one hand and the family's property on the other. To adopt someone from outside the *oikos* was usually contrary to those goals.

In uncommon situations—such as when a couple was unable to adopt a son or the boy they adopted perished in childhood—the law offered a loophole that allowed a family's bloodline and property to survive through a daughter. Such a young woman was called an *epikleros* in Athens and possibly in some other city-states. When her father passed away, she was obliged to marry a male relative, often an uncle or cousin. In this way the dead father's property stayed within the extended family.

Childhood and Education

For a majority of ancient Greek children, the atmosphere in which they grew up was, by today's standards, not very nurturing and even borderline abusive. They commonly received beatings with leather straps and wooden rods, for example. Moreover, the overall societal view of children was largely unconcerned with concepts like making them happy or building up their self-esteem and confidence. Indeed, childhood was not viewed as a memorable period in one's life, and most adults harbored few—if any—wistful thoughts about their youth.

Tradition, bolstered by successive generations of Greek thinkers, held that children were nearly worthless in and of themselves. They lacked the power to reason, the argument went. They were also destructive, undisciplined, and bereft of both courage and a sense of morality until they were at least in their teens. Therefore, adults must closely watch and harshly discipline them. "Of all animals," Plato stated, "the boy is the most unmanageable" because "his fountain of reason is not yet regulated." That "is why he must be bound with many bridles. In the first place, when he gets away from mothers and nurses, he must be under the

A teacher guides his student in a writing lesson. Boys from wealthy families started school at the age of seven or eight and studied reading, writing, music, athletics, and dancing.

management of tutors on account of his childishness and foolishness."[17]

Still, Greek children's lives were not completely miserable. They did play with toys, including many familiar today—dolls, hoops, balls, yo-yos, and so forth. Also common were miniature houses, wagons, and chariots. In addition, large numbers of children had pets. Paintings on surviving cups and other pottery objects illustrate both boys and girls playing with dogs, ducks, mice, and other small creatures.

As children grew, there was increasingly less time for play, however. Boys in poorer farm families frequently had to begin helping their fathers with chores before they were ten. Meanwhile, in better-off families young boys started going to school at age seven or eight. Their sisters were generally taught weaving, sewing, and other household arts by their mothers.

The schools where boys learned reading, writing, music, and physical education (athletic events and dancing) were private and paid for by their parents. The classes were usually held in informal spaces—rooms in the backs of houses or attached to local gyms—rather than in separate school buildings. It was fairly common for a boy's parents to have a slave called a *paidagogos* walk him to school and supervise his behavior there. If the child acted up, that overseer had permission to discipline him appropriately.

Household Slaves and Their Jobs

The role of *paidagogos* was just one of numerous jobs done by slaves in and around Greek homes. Slavery was never as prevalent in Greece as it eventually became in Rome, which had by far the largest slavery institution in the ancient world. Nevertheless, slaves did much of the unskilled and boring labor in the Greek lands.

As was the case with other ancient peoples, the Greeks saw slavery as part of the natural order of life. The general consensus was that the gods themselves fully accepted the concept of slavery. Likewise, the most esteemed thinkers of the era—brilliant individuals like Plato and Aristotle—could not conceive of a society that ran efficiently without the use of slave labor. Moreover, even the slaves bought into this way of thinking. This is demonstrated by the fact that many of them who managed to earn their freedom immediately acquired slaves of their own.

> **WORDS IN CONTEXT**
> *paidagogos*
> A Greek household slave assigned to accompany a boy to school and oversee his behavior there.

Most slaves who worked in Greek homes were non-Greeks, since the idea of Greeks enslaving fellow Greeks was widely frowned on. A major-

A Spartan overseer whips slaves as they plow a field. Laws in ancient Athens prohibited serious brutality against slaves but in Sparta slaves were often treated with extreme cruelty.

ity of household slaves were people purchased from slave traders or captured in wars. Lesser numbers were bred in the home, and those tended to be viewed more or less as part of the family. The number of slaves who lived and worked in Greek homes is unclear. But modern experts have made various estimates. Based on these estimates, a household of average means likely had two to five slaves, and a well-to-do family may have had fifteen, twenty, or more.

The female household slaves aided their mistress and her daughters (if any) with cooking, cleaning, spinning, weaving, and sewing. Women slaves also nursed babies and helped supervise the family children. In some situations a slave woman might manage an entire household for her owner. This typically happened when the owner was well-to-do and had a country house requiring upkeep when he and his family were living in town.

Meanwhile, on country farms the male slaves performed agricultural jobs, including planting, harvesting, threshing, pruning, and caring for the livestock. Frequently, these slaves worked side by side with their owners. In townhouses in the urban areas, by comparison, male slaves did home repairs and ran errands and carried messages for the master. They also went grocery shopping in the agora (or helped the master do it), acted as *paidagogos* for the master's son, and chaperoned the family women when they appeared in public. In addition, on rare occasions—a national emergency for instance—the male slaves fought at their masters' sides in battle.

Treatment of Slaves

Some household slaves were treated badly by unkind masters, but this tended to be the exception rather than the rule. In most cases both custom and law prevented serious brutality. Furthermore, in Athens it was a crime for a free person to beat or kill another citizen's slave, and it was illegal for a master to kill his own slave no matter what offense the slave had committed.

Instead, an owner who had problems with a slave was required to follow the law. In a court speech delivered around 419 BCE, an Athenian told the jury, "Even slaves who kill their masters, even if they are caught red-handed, are not [allowed to be] put to death by the relatives of the deceased. The relatives hand them over to the authorities in accordance with [Athens's] laws."[18]

Thus, household slaves were generally well treated in Athens and presumably most other Greek states. Indeed, some of these live-in servants became almost like members of the family. The most trusted ones received small wages, better described as tips, for their good behavior. A slave was allowed to spend this money or save it up and use it to purchase his or her freedom. (The freeing of a slave was called manumission.)

The most glaring exception to this overall humane treatment of slaves was in Sparta, again a maverick among the majority of Greek states. Before the dawn of the Classical era, the Spartans conquered the neighboring Greek polis of Messenia and enslaved its inhabitants. Called *helots*, these Spartan slaves did backbreaking work from sunup to sundown and were treated with extreme cruelty.

> **WORDS IN CONTEXT**
> **manumission**
> The act or procedure of freeing a slave.

In Their Own Words

An Argument Supporting Slavery

The renowned fourth-century-BCE thinker Aristotle was one of many ancient writers who argued that slavery was perfectly natural and just. In his treatise titled *Politics*, he mentions a minority of thinkers who believe "that the rule of a master over slaves is contrary to nature," and is therefore unjust. However, Aristotle says, this view is in error because a slave is only a tool, or instrument. "Instruments," he explains,

> are of various sorts. Some are living, others lifeless. In the rudder, the pilot of a ship has a lifeless [instrument], and in the look-out man, a living instrument. For in the arts, a servant is a kind of instrument. Thus, too, a possession is an instrument for maintaining life. And so, in the arrangement of the family, a slave is a living possession. . . . Hence we see what is the nature and office of a slave. He who is by nature not his own but another's man, is by nature a slave. And he may be said to be another's man who, being a slave, is also a possession. And a possession may be defined as an instrument of action, separable from the possessor. . . . That some should rule and others *be* ruled is a thing not only necessary, but expedient. From the hour of their birth, some are marked out for subjection, others for rule.

Aristotle, *Politics*, trans. Benjamin Jowett, in *The Complete Works of Aristotle*, vol. 2, ed. Jonathan Barnes. Princeton: Princeton University Press, 1984, pp. 1989–90.

Fortunately for the helots, near the close of Classical times a Theban army soundly defeated the Spartans. The victors freed the long-suffering Messenians, who rebuilt their shattered city-state. One might say that, from the standpoint of people in later ages looking back on ancient Greek life, the worst stain on its otherwise impressive reputation was thereby removed.

Chapter Three

Community Life
and Religion

The citizens of the Greek states in the Classical period had certain expected community responsibilities and roles. One of the foremost of those public duties—taking part in local government—was unwritten, in the sense that no law said everyone had to do it. However, it became a kind of badge of patriotism, honor, and decency for a man (as women were generally excluded from politics) to get involved, even if only once in his lifetime.

In addition to the many government positions available, there were hundreds of positions and jobs that kept the community functioning smoothly on a regular basis. Among them were helping maintain the streets, marketplaces, and other public facilities. Also, Athens—and probably most of the other larger city-states—had a system of public contributions called liturgies. The state kept a list of the well-to-do members of the community; each year, in a rotation system, some of them stepped forward to pay for various community needs. Some of these included distributing food at religious festivals, supporting theatrical productions, erecting statues and monuments, and paying the singers and dancers who performed at public festivals.

In addition, some of those community sponsors made key contributions of money and time to Athens's navy. Every year, each of a few hundred wealthy men outfitted and maintained one warship (called a *trireme*) for that season. The following year, a different group of well-off citizens provided that service, and the state's contribution was to provide the ships and pay the rowers.

Similarly, those rowers manned their oars as a way of doing their own community service. Each year, in Athens and the other city-states that had navies, hundreds and in some cases thousands of men signed up to be oarsmen on state warships. The rowers were not slaves, as often incorrectly depicted in Hollywood movies. Rather, they were free men who came mainly from the lower classes.

Another major portion of community life was built around religion. It included erecting and maintaining temples and other shrines dedicated to the gods, and serving as priests who were usually ordinary people who led public sacrifices and other forms of worship. Community religious life also consisted of organizing yearly public religious festivals, contributing animals for mass sacrifices during those festivals, and taking part in them on a regular basis. The belief was that such acts not only pleased the gods but also supported one's community and fellow citizens.

The Path to Democracy

These and similar examples of community life and service existed in all Greek city-states. But they were particularly prevalent in democracies. A brief examination of how democracy developed in Greece shows how the institutions and public positions that dominated community life came to be. Most of the evidence comes from Athens, partly because it created the world's first true democracy.

This great milestone in human history, which took place in 508 BCE, was the result of close to two centuries of political unrest and experimentation. Like other Greek states, Athens had once been ruled by king-like rulers. But the people objected to the concentration of too much power in the hands of a single person. So at some unknown date, they eliminated the king and replaced him with three public administrators called *archons*.

> **WORDS IN CONTEXT**
> *archon*
> An administrative post in many ancient Greek governments. Archons were similar to selectmen, mayors, and councilors in modern town governments.

Initially, the archons served for life. But in the seventh century BCE, the people, collectively called the *demos*, demanded that new archons be

Residents of ancient Athens honor Athena, the goddess of war and wisdom. Religious festivals and processions were a regular feature of Greek life.

chosen each year by election. Once the people realized their power to instigate positive change in their community, there was no turning back on the path toward democracy. Soon six more archons were added. It appears that all nine were elected by the Assembly, or *Ecclesia*, a group of landholders who met to choose community leaders.

The next hurdle on that path to democracy involved community laws. Legal concepts and notions of right and wrong had long existed. But they were mostly in the form of traditions and not written down, so the archons could decide court cases and resolve community disputes any way they saw fit. Once again the *demos* objected to this unfair abuse of power and insisted that the laws be written down. Not wanting to tangle with an angry citizenry, the archons appointed a man named Draco to do that. His laws turned out to be way too strict, with overly harsh penalties. So by the early 500s BCE, Athens's general population was again dissatisfied and demanding political reform.

Hoping to avoid the possibility of a violent revolution, in 594 BCE both sides asked a citizen with a reputation for honesty, fairness, and wisdom—Solon—to step in. His solution was radical but brilliant. First, he threw out most of Draco's repressive laws. He also created the Council, or *Boule*, a group of four hundred men chosen by lot, or random drawing. Their task was to prepare an agenda, a list of community issues needing immediate attention. The councilors passed this list on to the Assembly, whose members debated and voted on the issues it contained. Solon summarized his achievement, saying, "To the mass of the people I gave the power they needed, neither degrading them, nor giving them too much rein.

For those who already possessed great power and wealth I saw to it that their interests were not harmed. I stood guard with a broad shield before both parties and prevented either from triumphing unjustly."[19]

Community Services in Democracies

Although he did not realize it, Solon had laid the groundwork for full-blown democracy. The final step occurred in 508 BCE when an influential Athenian leader named Cleisthenes overhauled both the city-state and its government. Despite previous reforms, much authority in the community rested behind the scenes in the traditional, powerful influence of a few wealthy families. Cleisthenes smashed their authority and influence. He also increased membership in the Council from four hundred to five hundred and assured that the members of that body represented all social classes.

In this way Cleisthenes set in motion a democratic system that the Athenian *demos* would continue to expand and make even more liberal in the years that followed. The new system operated on the principle of *isonomia*, meaning "equality under the law." Noted historian Michael Grant explains, "The *isonomia* of Cleisthenes was a sophisticated, intricate, and experimental array of new political institutions, adding up to the most democratic form of government that had so far been devised by human ingenuity, and establishing the essential features of Athenian society for 200 years."[20]

In fact, even up to the present day, human ingenuity has yet to devise a democracy as pure and open as that initial one that appeared in Athens. In part this is because modern democracies are nations with millions of inhabitants. For example, it is physically impossible for the more than 100 million Americans eligible to vote to gather in a single meeting, debate the issues, and vote on them on the spot. In Athens and other Greek democracies, in contrast, the citizenry numbered in the thousands. So in most cases all eligible voters *could* assemble in one place.

> **WORDS IN CONTEXT**
> *isonomia*
> Equality under the law.

This fact is essential to understanding everyday community life and duties in many of the Greek states. On a regular basis, every free male citizen who desired to attend his local assembly did so. In Athens, for instance, a man of any social class could raise his hand or voice in that meeting and quite literally address the nation. Then, along with the others, he could vote. The results of these votes did much more than select community leaders. They also established both domestic and foreign policy. The foreign policy was then carried out by ten elected statesmen, the *strategoi*, or generals, called that because they also commanded the army and navy in wartime.

Ostracism and Jury Service

Ordinary Athenian citizens could also wake up in the morning, get dressed, walk to the Agora or other meeting place, and without delay kick leaders they disliked out of office. This was possible because of a special democratic process called ostracism. The citizens brought with them pieces of broken pottery called *ostraka*. On them, one modern expert says, "they had scratched the name of the man they felt represented a threat to the democracy. The man with the most votes lost and he was exiled for ten years. In the early years of the fifth century BCE, most of

In Their Own Words

The Art of Oratory

At the core of ancient Greek democracy was the power of both leaders and ordinary people to express themselves to their fellow citizens in public. This was especially true in the meetings of an assembly like the one in Athens. Usually only the most eloquent speakers could sway the masses and impose their ideas on them. In this excerpt from his biography of Pericles, the first-century-CE Greek writer Plutarch tells about that great leader's mastery of public speaking.

> He [Pericles] had acquired, in addition to his natural gifts, what the divine Plato calls "the loftiness of thought and the power to create an ideally perfect work," and by applying this training to the art of oratory he far excelled all other speakers. This was the reason, some people say, for his being nicknamed the Olympian, though others believe it was on account of the buildings with which he adorned Athens, and others again because of his prowess as a statesman and a general. But it may well have been the combination of many qualities which earned him the name. However, the comic poets of the time, who were constantly letting fly at [criticizing] him either in earnest or in fun, declare that the title originated mainly from his manner of speaking. They refer to him as thundering and lightning when he addressed his audience and as wielding a terrible thunderbolt in his tongue.

Plutarch, *Life of Pericles*, in "Plutarch," *The Rise and Fall of Athens: Nine Greek Lives*, trans. Ian Scott-Kilvert. New York: Penguin, 1983, p. 172.

the prominent Athenian politicians took one of these enforced ten-year vacations, courtesy of the Athenian people."[21]

The number of other Greek poleis that installed the procedure of ostracism, if any, is unknown. What is more certain is that a fairly substantial proportion of city-states followed the Athenian lead and set up their own democracies. Moreover, those city-states that did not institute full-blown democracy usually had a modified form of it. Or they had various kinds of representative government, such as councils of elders who were expected to carry out the wishes of the general citizenry. Even Sparta, which thoroughly distrusted Athens's open democracy, had a council of elders.

The choices that citizens in many of these states had for community service and duties were large. In addition to councils, assemblies, boards of statesmen-generals, liturgies to take care of community needs, rowers for the ships, and similar jobs and institutions, there were courts with juries. These were not the sort of juries seen most often in modern democracies—with six to twelve members. In comparison, juries in ancient Greece were huge.

In Athens, for instance, each year six thousand men who were at least thirty years old were on call to be jurors. (As in the case of voting and holding public office, women were not allowed to be jurors.) Most of these men looked forward to serving. But at first, many of the poorest ones were unable to do so because they could not afford to miss work during the days or weeks a trial was in session. To remedy that unfortunate flaw, the government instigated a policy of paying jurors a daily fee. That did more than ensure that even the poorest Athenians who wanted to serve could do so. The fee was also a kind of old-age pension for elderly folk.

Other Forms of Community Life

Working in and for the government or aiding the polis in other material ways occupied men's hours outside the home more than any other single kind of activity. Yet there were numerous other communal pursuits that men, and sometimes women, engaged in fairly regularly. One was shopping for food, clothes, luxury goods, and other items.

Because Athens was the biggest, richest, and most influential city-state,

Male citizens of Athens gather at the Agora for a vote to ostracize a fellow citizen. If citizens felt a politician threatened their democracy, they could vote to exile him from Athens for a ten-year period.

it had the most impressive array of goods for sale in shops and the marketplace. However, several other prosperous states—including Corinth, Argos, and Thebes on the mainland and island poleis like Aegina, Naxos, and Chios—also carried a wide variety of wares from across the known world. Only a few of these were papyrus (for making paper) from Egypt; linen from Syria; pork and aged cheeses from Syracuse (in Sicily); ivory from North Africa; dates from Phoenicia (along the eastern Mediterranean coast); and wheat from the vast fields lying west and north of the Black Sea.

In addition to these foreign commodities, the city-states themselves produced numerous useful goods. A partial list includes vegetables, fruit, and fish; clothes, hats, and shoes; urns, vases, tableware, and all manner of other pottery items; and jewelry made of copper, bronze, gold, and silver.

Before going shopping, one had to make sure he or she had the proper currency. In the Classical era, especially the second half, gold and silver coins were the norm. The most widely accepted coins were Athenian silver drachmas (nicknamed "owls" because they displayed an image of that bird); coins made of electrum (a mixture of gold and silver) from Cyzicus, a Greek state located near the Black Sea's entrance; and darics, gold coins from the Persian Empire, which then covered most of the Middle East.

Anyone who possessed local coins, jewelry, or other valuables that were not widely accepted as currency usually had to exchange them for more acceptable coins. Almost every larger polis had private bankers who acted as money changers. By custom, they set up their tables outside temples and of course in marketplaces, where they charged a rate of 6 percent for doing the exchange.

Once a shopper had the right coins, he or she went to the shops or vendors of choice. In most city-states, the majority of goods for sale were in the local agoras. But the shops of local craftsmen could be found mixed in with other buildings along a town's narrow, winding streets. Many merchants, particularly in the agoras, had more portable shops consisting of awning-covered wagons packed with their goods.

In addition to shopping, communal activities for men frequently included going to a local gym to work out and/or enjoy informal wrestling matches. There and in adjacent fields, some men trained for upcoming athletic competitions, including the famous Olympic Games. Some of those same men could sometimes be seen on street corners or elsewhere debating the hottest issues of the day with fellow citizens. Still another popular communal activity—open to women as well as men—was the theater. The most famous theater facility was in Athens, but numerous others were erected across the Greek lands during Classical times.

The Importance of Religion

Of all the diverse forms of community life, religious worship was the oldest and most deeply rooted in tradition. Most Greeks were very pious, so they took the various ceremonies of public worship seriously. Public religion was also widely seen as vital to the polis's security, since neglecting the gods might insult them and bring down divine wrath on the community.

Marketplaces throughout Greece offered a wide variety of items for shoppers. These included pottery of various shapes and sizes; vegetables, fruit, and fish; clothing, hats, and shoes; and jewelry crafted from copper, gold, silver, and bronze.

Religious rituals took place at virtually every public gathering. Before a feast, for example, the diners offered some of the food to the gods. Similarly, assembly meetings started out with animal sacrifices and prayers; a military general sacrificed a goat or other creature directly before a battle; and prayers to the gods preceded speeches in the law courts. Demosthenes's most famous speech, *On the Crown*, delivered to a jury in 330 BCE, started with a religious invocation. "I begin, men of Athens" he said, "by praying to every god and goddess" for sentiments of goodwill. After calling on the gods to come to his aid, he asked them to direct the jury "to such a decision upon this indictment [prosecution] as will contribute to your common honor, and to the good conscience of each individual."[22]

The Greeks also thought that religious devotion and patriotism went hand in hand. The common view was that a god or gods could show favor to one city-state above many or all others. "The gods are quite evidently on our side now," an Athenian soldier is recorded as saying in the midst of war. "In the middle of fair weather they send a snowstorm to help us, and when we attack, few against many, it is we who are granted the right to set up the trophies [victory monuments]."[23]

Human-Like Gods

Having the support of the gods had a cost, however, since the Greeks believed the gods demanded something in return. That *something* consisted of worship, which had many facets. Besides prayer, they included sacrifices, erecting shrines to the deities, celebrating yearly festivals in their honor, and speaking directly to those divinities through oracles. The latter were priestesses who, it was thought, acted as mediums between humans and the gods.

Chief among these deities were the so-called Olympians. That title derived from an old tradition that held that they resided atop Mount Olympus, in the mainland's northern sector. Not only is it the highest peak on the mainland, its summit is frequently sheathed in thick clouds, giving it an imposing, mysterious air. By the Classical Age, however, most people realized that no one, mortal or immortal, dwelled on the mountain. Instead, the common belief became that the gods lived in an invisible realm located somewhere in the sky.

The supreme leader of that celestial realm was Zeus, whose most popular symbols were the thunderbolt, oak tree, and eagle. His divine wife, Hera, whose symbols were the peacock and pomegranate, protected marriage and children. According to numerous Greek myths, she also fumed with jealousy over her husband's many affairs with goddesses and human women alike.

Also, Zeus's brothers, Poseidon and Hades, had charge of major regions of the natural world. Poseidon ruled the seas, often brandishing one of his symbols, the trident (three-pronged spear), or riding another—the dolphin. Hades, meanwhile, ruled the Underworld, the land of the dead. Some of the other major Olympians included Apollo, god of prophecy, healing, and music; his twin sister, Artemis, mistress of the moon, wild animals, and hunting; Ares, god of war; and Athena, the deity of wisdom and war.

In ancient Greek eyes, these majestic beings possessed human form and human-like emotions, as well as having marriages and children, just as humans did. Other than immortality, the primary trait that separated gods and people was the immense power those deities wielded. The common belief was that this power could either aid and support human civilization or demolish it. As the fifth-century-BCE Greek poet Pindar aptly put it, "Single [is] the race, single of men and gods. From a single mother we both draw breath. But a difference of power in everything keeps us apart."[24]

> **WORDS IN CONTEXT**
> **trident**
> A three-pronged spear made famous as a symbol of Poseidon, the Greek god who ruled the seas.

The Most Devout

Although most Greeks recognized and respected all the gods, each city-state had a patron deity—a divinity that supposedly favored and protected that state and its people. In exchange for such protection, the city provided its patron with his or her own house or shelter—a temple. Athens, for instance, erected a number of temples to its beloved patron, Athena. Among these structures was the renowned Parthenon, the ruins of which still stand on the towering Acropolis, in Athens's center.

Typically, a statue of the local patron god, called a cult image, rested inside a temple. The belief was that the deity sometimes actually lived there, so to respect his or her privacy no major worship took place inside. Instead, public ceremonies occurred at altars set up on the building's steps or elsewhere on the property.

The central feature of these ceremonies was the act of sacrifice, in which goats, sheep, and other animals were ritually slaughtered. After

Looking Back

Greek Visions of the Afterlife

All through their ancient history, almost all Greeks believed in an afterlife. The only notable exception was the philosophy of the Epicureans, who held that the human soul died along with the body. Still, not every Greek saw the afterlife the same way. According to historian David Sacks:

> Because Greek religion had no specific doctrine on the subject, beliefs in the afterlife varied greatly, from crude superstition to the philosopher Plato's lofty vision of an immortal soul freed of its imperfect flesh and at one with absolute reality in another world. The primitive concept that the dead somehow live on in their tombs never disappeared from Greek religion. . . . The general idea seems to have survived in Greece for over 1,000 years. Greeks of the 400s and 300s BCE were still offering food and drink at graveside, as nourishment for the dead. Another belief was that the souls of the dead traveled to an Underworld, the realm of the god Hades and his wife Persephone. Unlike the modern concept of Hell, this "House of Hades" (as the Greeks called it) was not primarily a place of punishment. It was, however, a cold and gloomy setting, where the souls—after being led from the living world by the messenger god Hermes—endured a bleak eternity.

David Sacks, *Encyclopedia of the Ancient Greek World*. New York: Fact On File, 1995, pp. 8–9.

a creature was killed, carefully following age-old rules, some body parts were burned to appease the gods. People thought that the smoke rose up into the deities' invisible kingdom and nourished them. The worshippers then cooked and ate the sacrificed animal's meat in sacred feasts. "The beasts were dragged before the altar," prominent scholar John Boardman writes, describing a typical Athenian public sacrifice.

> The stunning axe rose and fell, the knives lost their luster beneath a coat of fat and blood. The rock was slippery with blood, the air heavy with the smell of guts and sweat. The slaughter bred excitement, shouting anticipation of the feasts to come, while the black smoke rolled thick and heavy up into the still and shimmering air, a clear signal to Athena that her citizens had paid their due respect.[25]

These visually striking rituals were accompanied by other communal religious acts. Quite common were massive processions in which large portions of a polis's population took part. In Athens, for example, the marchers in Athena's biggest festival, the Panathenaea, represented all social classes and groups. There were even slaves, who led the beasts about to be sacrificed. All involved beamed with pride, as they felt they were serving both the goddess and their community.

A handful of citizens had no interest in marching in the holiday processions, nor in any other aspect of religion. As Plato wrote, a few members of society "do not believe at all in the existence of the gods."[26] But such individuals were by far the exception. Community life in ancient Greece was dominated by those who believed as Socrates did. "Can't you see," he asked (according to Xenophon), "that the most enduring and wise of all human beings are the most devout, and that the most intelligent times of life are the ones which are the most full of regard for the gods?"[27]

Chapter Four

Sports and Other Leisure Activities

In describing the ancient Greeks' unique spirit, the late, great classical scholar Edith Hamilton famously said that they "played on a great scale." She continued, "All over Greece there were games, all sorts of games: athletic contests of every description; races—horse, boat, foot, torch races; contests in music where one side out-sang the other, [and contests] in dancing." Indeed, there were "games so many that one grows weary with the list of them." Summing up in a dramatic flourish, Hamilton stated, "If we had no other knowledge of what the Greeks were like, if nothing were left of Greek art and literature, the fact that they were in love with play and played magnificently would be proof enough of how they lived and how they looked at life."[28]

Desperate to Win

A love for all sorts of sports and games was not the only factor that motivated the Greeks to engage in these activities. They also possessed a strong inner desire to compete, and especially to win. Historians used to think that Greek athletes were amateurs who competed mainly in a spirit of fellowship and because they viewed sports and competing in them as somehow noble. This is why in the 1890s the organizers of the modern Olympic Games excluded professional athletes and opened those contests to amateurs only.

But this theory proved to be mistaken. In the twentieth century proof emerged that the Greeks did not even recognize the modern idea of amateur sports. Indeed, they received hefty rewards for competing, which made them quite professional. Moreover, they were almost desperate to win first place, not just for the prizes, but more so for the glory—what they saw as everlasting fame. Part of the evidence for this is the fact that the losers frequently experienced shame and dejection. According to the poet Pindar, some of the losers in one major competition received "no glad homecoming." Rather, "when they meet their mothers," those young men "have no sweet laughter to cheer them up." Returning to their home towns, "they cower, avoiding their enemies. Disaster has bitten them."[29]

The Greeks called the extreme desire to be the best at something *aristos*. That concept went hand in hand with their word for "contest"—*agon*. It also meant "struggle" and was regularly used to describe battles and lawsuits. For the Greeks, therefore, there was a clearly forceful, serious side or edge to playing games.

> **WORDS IN CONTEXT**
> *aristos*
> The desire to be the best at something.

Still another reason the Greeks saw competing in athletic and other games as a serious matter was that most of those contests were held in honor of one or more gods. The athletes earnestly and solemnly dedicated their physical or creative skills to those deities. Winners could claim they had glorified a divinity, whereas losers sometimes felt they had disappointed the gods and therefore should hang their heads or shrink away.

Local and International Contests

Not only were taking part in and watching contests of various kinds, particularly athletic ones, a regular part of Greek life, so too was training for such events. It was only natural, then, that facilities for such training could be found in every town. This explains the development of local gyms, wrestling schools, and athletic fields, where men of all ages worked out, practiced diverse athletic events, and engaged in local competitions. (Women were not allowed to compete with men, but a separate female athletic contest was held every four years at Olympia. Also, far more than most other Greek women, Spartan women were encouraged to exercise regularly and become physically strong.) Such local competitions, which

Runners in Athens take part in a relay race that involves passing a lit torch from one team member to the next until the last runners reach the end of the course. Teams in these races sometimes had as many as forty runners.

to modern eyes seem like miniature versions of the Olympics, took place in virtually every Greek state. The biggest one, which drew spectators from many neighboring poleis, was the one staged annually at Athens.

Even the Athenian national games paled in prestige, however, compared to Greece's four largest athletic competitions. These were panhellenic (all-Greek), meaning they were open to Greeks everywhere. Each of these big four athletic gatherings honored a well-known god. The Olympic Games held at Olympia were the most exalted—partly because they were dedicated to the leading Greek deity, Zeus, and also because they were the oldest. But the others ran a close second. They were the Isthmian Games, honoring Poseidon, held every two years at his sanctuary on the Isthmus of Corinth; the Nemean Games, dedicated to Zeus, held at two-year intervals at Nemea (a few miles south of Corinth); and the Pythian Games, dedicated to Apollo, held at Delphi in the third year after each Olympics.

Judges and Events

More or less, the big four had the same kinds of events, as well as featured similar kinds of facilities for the athletes and spectators. Therefore, a look at the Olympics gives a fair idea of what the other three games were like. The Olympic Games were presented by the Eleans, the residents of the city-state of Elis, in which Olympia was situated. Every four years the town's elders chose the men who would oversee and judge the events. These judges, who wore purple robes, held a lot of authority. Indeed, they had the power to punish rule breakers harshly. A man caught cheating or taking bribes could be fined, flogged, or tossed out of the games, depending on the situation.

The program of events these judges supervised spanned five days. Included were horse and chariot races; the pentathlon (a combination of running, jumping, the discus throw, the javelin throw, and wrestling); footraces; the broad jump; combat sports (wrestling, boxing, and the *pankration*—similar to today's mixed martial arts); and running and wrestling events for boys between ages twelve and eighteen.

Many of these same events could also be found in the local games in the various city-states. However, each town had a few extra events usually not found anywhere else. Athens, for instance, had tribal torch races, one of which was a relay race in which each tribe had up to forty runners. Among the forty, each athlete ran about 200 feet (61 m) and then passed a lit torch to a teammate. That teammate also ran 200 feet and passed the torch, a process that continued over a course of more than 1.5 miles (2.4 km).

Dinner and Party Guests

These facts show clearly that Greek men thoroughly enjoyed athletics. Yet their enthusiasm was no less ardent for certain other leisure pastimes, including holding dinners for male friends. This is why so many townhouses had *androns*, private dining areas where male heads of families

In Their Own Words

Socrates and the Dancing Girl

In his work titled the *Symposium*, Xenophon describes entertainers he witnessed at a drinking party also attended by his friend and mentor, the philosopher Socrates. "When the dining tables were removed," Xenophon writes,

> a certain man from [the Greek city of] Syracuse came in to furnish entertainment, having as his assistants a girl skilled in playing the flute, a dancing girl marvelously adept at acrobatics, and a boy at the peak of his beauty, skilled in playing the lyre [a small harp] and in dancing. By exhibiting them in their marvelous performance, the owner earned a living. . . . [Soon Socrates said] "let us continue with the entertainment. For I see that the dancing girl has come out, and they are giving her some hoops." Thereupon, one girl played the flute for her, and someone else standing beside the dancer kept giving her hoops until she had twelve. As she danced, she threw them into the air, making them spin, and judging how high she would have to throw them to catch them in time to the music. And Socrates said, "In what this girl is doing and in many other respects is proof that woman's nature is not at all inferior to man's, but it needs strength and force. And so those of you who have wives, be encouraged to teach them whatever you would like them to know."

Xenophon, "Symposium," trans. Waldo E. Sweet, in *Sport and Recreation in Ancient Greece*, ed. Waldo E. Sweet. New York: Oxford University Press, 1987, pp. 203–204.

entertained. On those occasions, female members of the family retired to the so-called women's quarters, situated either upstairs or in the back of the house. One reason that women were excluded from such banquets was that men, and society in general, frowned on allowing wives and daughters to socialize with men from outside the extended family.

Observing polite custom, the dinner guests removed their shoes upon arrival. (Streets were usually filthy with litter, garbage, and animal droppings.) If the host owned slaves, they cleaned the guests' feet and escorted them into the *andron*. Those same slaves served the food, bringing it in large bowls that sat on small, portable tables. Often the guests reclined on their sides on couches, each using either a pillow or one elbow to prop up his upper body.

As for table manners, the guests ate most food items with their hands. Obvious exceptions were soup and pudding, for which the servers brought out spoons. Also, the diners tossed peach and cherry pits, chicken bones, and other scraps onto the floor, which the servants cleaned up the next morning.

Another common practice was to follow such a meal with an after-dinner drinking party called a symposium. Although most of the wine was diluted with water in the customary way, at least some of the guests were apt to drink too much. This fact is revealed in the works of several ancient writers, including Plato. In his appropriately named dialogue, the *Symposium*, he depicts an Athenian drinking party that his mentor, the thinker Socrates, attended.

> **WORDS IN CONTEXT**
> *cottabos*
> A popular drinking-party game in which the players hurled the residue from their wine cups at something in the room.

Plato and other writers also described typical activities the guests at symposia enjoyed. These included telling stories and riddles, making offerings to the gods, singing songs, and playing party games. As one of the characters attending the symposium described by Plato says, "We poured offerings, sang hymns, and did all the usual things. Then our thoughts turned to drinking."[30] Of the party games, a particularly popular one was known as *cottabos*. The players attempted to fling the wine dregs, or residue, from the bottoms of their cups at a spot on a wall or some other

Party guests fling the wine dregs from their cups at a target in the center of the room. The game, called cottabos, *was popular at Athenian drinking parties.*

target in the room. In one case the target was a water-filled bowl in which some small clay saucers floated. "The game then consisted in aiming at these miniscule 'boats,'" Robert Flaceliere writes, "and throwing the wine so skillfully that it made them overturn and sink. The *cottabos* prize went to whoever caused the largest number of 'shipwrecks.'"[31]

In addition, hosts who could afford it brought in entertainers of various sorts, among them musicians, dancers, and even acrobats. Xenophon, who also penned a work titled the *Symposium*, recalled witnessing a female pipe player, a woman acrobatic dancer, and a boy who played the harp. Xenophon wrote that the dancer put on an impressive show as she threw several large hoops "spinning up into the air as she danced."[32]

Music and Dancing

Music played a part in numerous other aspects of Greek life besides symposia. Religious processions and festivities, weddings and funerals, birth celebrations and clan gatherings, stage plays, and formal musical competitions all featured musicians. Even war proved a venue for music, a famous example being the flute players who accompanied Spartan soldiers on the battlefield. Besides flutes, Greek musicians played harps of varying size, drums, tambourines, and trumpets.

One of the largest and most impressive musical presentations was the victory ode, created for the winner of an athletic event. In some cases a small orchestra of musicians played, accompanied by a choir of singers. Pindar was the master of this kind of victory ode. The lyrics, or words, to several of his odes have survived, although the tunes themselves have not.

Aside from the athletes, the musicians also competed against one another. One of the odes Pindar wrote for a prize-winning musician named Midas has luckily survived the ravages of time. "Take this Pythian wreath [of victory] achieved by glorious Midas," it reads in part. "And take himself, victor of Greece, in that art [of music] which Athena invented."[33]

As one would expect, Greek music also provided the beat for dancers. There were traditional dances of all kinds in the Greek lands, including those that took place onstage in local theaters, at religious celebrations, weddings, feasts, and harvest festivals. Among the vivid names of these dances that have survived are "Knocking at the Door," "The Itch," "Stealing the Meat," "Setting the World on Fire," and "The Piglet." Regrettably, the manner in which these dances were performed has *not* survived.

Attending the Theater

Music and dancing were regular features of theatrical presentations. The theater itself was one of the most popular leisure activities in ancient Greece, an institution and tradition enjoyed by all of a city-state's citizens and possibly in some states even by slaves. (Scholars still debate about attendance by slaves.)

The theater was invented and enjoyed its greatest ancient artistic flowering in Athens in the amazingly short period lasting from about 530 to 400 BCE. It remains a bit sketchy exactly how drama and theater appeared, but modern experts think they grew out of *dithyramb*. These were verses initially involved in the rituals connected to the worship of Dionysus, god of fertility and the vine. Later, dithyramb for other gods developed.

WORDS IN CONTEXT
dithyramb
Verses describing the life and exploits of the fertility god Dionysus and other deities.

Over time, worshippers came to sing and dance to the verses, which described those deities' lives and exploits. Then at some point a line was crossed whereby a priest reciting and singing the dithyramb became a sort of actor and the worshippers became his audience. "After that," in Aristotle's words, the evolution of full-fledged plays performed on stages "was little by little, through their improving on whatever they had before them at each stage. It was in fact only after a long series of changes that the [development] of tragedy [reached its present] form."[34]

At first, people from neighboring states traveled to Athens to attend plays in the Theater of Dionysus, erected at the base of the Acropolis. But during the fifth century BCE, theaters appeared in many other Greek towns. All accepted certain conventions, or traditional procedures and rules, one of the most important of which was the use of masks. By wearing masks of stock characters—like a fair young maiden or evil king—one actor could portray two or more characters in the same play. (All of the actors were men, as society viewed it as unseemly for women to display themselves in public that way.) Other stage conventions included costumes worn by the actors and props such as shields, swords, couches, torches, and so forth.

Play presentation usually began in the morning and lasted all day. When the spectators entered the theater, which was open to the elements, they sat in a semicircular area with ascending rows of stone seats. Called the *theatron*, or "viewing place," it faced the circular stage. Behind the stage stood the rectangular *skene*, or "scene building," which also served as a scenic backing for the story, a dressing room for the actors, and storage area for props.

When the audience was in place, city officials sacrificed a bull to satisfy the god Dionysus. Then the first play commenced. Most of these dramas were tragedies, whose stories came mainly from mythology and dealt with serious subjects, such as human relationships with the gods, morality, betrayal, and murder. Comedies gave audiences emotional relief from the bleakness of the tragic plays. The comic plays also offered a crucial outlet for political expression by poking fun at institutions and leaders. One historian comments, "In no other place or age were men of all classes attacked and ridiculed in public and by name with such

Theatrical masks (pictured in this relief depicting the Greek dramatist Menander) allowed one actor to portray several different characters in the same play. Actors also wore costumes and used props such as shields, swords, and couches.

freedom."[35] The audience members also had considerable freedom to express themselves during the performances. They laughed aloud, clapped, hissed at the villains, and consumed refreshments sold at the theater, much as modern baseball fans do during a game.

Ball Games and Hunting

Although the Greeks did not have the modern sport of baseball, they did enjoy a wide range of ball games. One popular game was highly recommended for staying in shape by the famous second-century-CE Greek physician Galen. "You need no nets, no weapons, no horses, no

65

hounds," he wrote, but rather, "just a single ball, and a small one at that." In playing it, he went on, a person could "move all the parts of the body equally." For example, when "people face each other, vigorously attempting to prevent each other from taking the space between, the exercise is a very heavy, vigorous one, involving much use of the hold by the neck, and many wrestling holds."[36]

The exact object and rules of the game Galen mentions here are unknown. But he may have been talking about a Greek team sport called *phaininda*. Apparently, it was a rough-and-tumble, rugby-like game in which members of the opposing teams exerted much energy trying to keep possession of the ball.

> **WORDS IN CONTEXT**
> *phaininda*
> A rough-and-tumble ball game that seems to have been similar to modern rugby.

Although evidence shows that the Greeks played some ball games well before the dawn of the Classical period, another vigorous pastime, hunting, was undoubtedly far older. The Greeks, like other ancient peoples, sometimes hunted to acquire extra food. But it eventually became a sport, too, especially among the well-to-do, who could afford hunting dogs, horses, elaborate traps, and slaves and servants to set up the traps and make and break camp.

Hunters routinely employed spears, knives, bows and arrows, slings, nets, and even clubs and sticks, depending on the situation and animals hunted—but trapping seems to have been the most common method. In his treatise on hunting, Xenophon mentions a spring trap he claims was often successful in bagging deer and other large prey. Pit traps were also popular. The hunter dug a deep hole with steep sides and placed thin branches and leaves over it. Then, when the deer or other creature stepped onto these materials, they gave way, causing the animal to fall into the pit.

A Love Affair with Play and Life

One of the chief attractions of hunting was that it transpired in the so-called great outdoors and gave a person the chance to challenge and overcome a particular aspect of nature. Another leisure activity that offered a similar challenge was mountain climbing. Unlike modern mountain climbers, however, most Greeks did not scale peaks merely to overcome that challenge and conquer nature. Mainland Greece was and remains

Looking Back

The Sacred Truce

One of the highlights of the Olympic Games in ancient Greece was the renowned Olympic truce. Every four years, three heralds from Elis—the so-called Truce Bearers—rode on horseback to every Greek state. Their task was to announce specific days during which the upcoming games would be held and to invite all to attend. They also proclaimed the sacred Olympic truce, or *ekecheiria*, described here by Judith Swaddling, an expert on the ancient Olympics:

> Originally, the Truce lasted for one month, but it was extended to two and then three months, to protect visitors coming from further afield. The terms of the Truce were engraved on a bronze discus which was kept in the Temple of Hera in the Altis [the sacred grounds of Zeus's temple at Olympia]. It forbade states participating in the Games to take up arms, to pursue legal disputes, or to carry out death penalties. This was to ensure that pilgrims and athletes traveling to and from Olympia would have a safe journey. Violators of the Truce were heavily fined, and indeed on one occasion, Alexander the Great himself had to recompense [pay damages to] an Athenian who was robbed by some of his mercenaries while traveling to Olympia.

Judith Swaddling, *The Ancient Olympic Games.* Austin: University of Texas Press, 1996, p. 12.

an extremely mountainous land. That forced many Greeks to regularly ascend steep hillsides simply to tend their livestock or visit a town in a neighboring valley. As a result, the Greeks "considered the mountains an abominable mistake of nature," in scholar Waldo E. Sweet's words. "Very few [Greeks] climbed a mountain 'because it was there,' as the modern cliché has it. If one did climb a peak, it was by the easiest route."[37]

Still, Sweet admits, at least a few Greeks did climb mountains to take pleasure in the superb views from the summit. How prevalent this was in the Classical Age is unknown. But in later ancient times, when Rome ruled the Greek states, Greeks and Romans alike enjoyed hikes to the tops of several well-known peaks. The first-century-BCE Greek traveler Strabo wrote about one of those mountains—the volcano Etna, in Sicily—where many Greeks still lived. He noted that the local authorities had created trails, lookouts, huts to allow climbers to rest or stay overnight, and other similar amenities.

Strabo added that Mount Etna attracted numerous tourists, including Greeks like himself, from across the Mediterranean sphere. Catering to those travelers, he said, "a small village called Etna takes in climbers and sends them on their way, for the ridge of the mountain begins here. Those who had recently climbed to the summit told me that at the top was a level plain,"[38] formed by dried lava.

Whether it was training for athletic competitions, applauding masterfully written plays in the theater, or soaking up the grandeur of nature, the Greeks continued their love affair with both play and life in general. "To rejoice in life," Edith Hamilton remarked, "to find the world beautiful and delightful to live in, was a mark of the Greek spirit, which distinguished it from all that had gone before." Indeed, "the joy of life is written upon everything the Greeks left behind," and this is vital "in understanding how the Greek achievement came to pass."[39]

Chapter Five

Patriotism, Warfare, and Survival

The fact that the Greek city-states were tiny independent nations had a major, ongoing effect not only on their long-term destinies, but also on the everyday lives of their inhabitants. There were hundreds of these states on the Greek mainland alone, each very protective of its interests. Not surprisingly, therefore, territorial, political, and other differences among neighboring states were common, and small-scale warfare was frequent. During the Classical Age, for example, Athens was at war with one party or another fully three-quarters of the time.

Also, the Greek mainland and nearby islands were tempting targets for foreign conquerors. In the first century or so of the Classical period, the chief threat in this regard was the Persian Empire, spanning most of the Middle East. The world's largest and strongest realm during those years, Persia continually lurked nearby as Greece's leading foreign foe.

Farmers in Armor

As a consequence of these very real threats of war, the tiny Greek nation-states had to be able to defend themselves almost on a moment's notice. Significantly, the populations of these states were generally very small. That meant that a majority of a polis's able-bodied men had to belong to a local militia. A part-time and temporary army, in an emergency its members grabbed their weapons, fought a battle, and then returned to their jobs and lives when the crisis was over.

With few exceptions, those militiamen were farmers and other male citizens who in wartime doubled as heavily armored infantrymen (foot soldiers) called *hoplites*. This was especially logical and fitting in democratic-leaning states. After all, these men were usually the voters in the assemblies who determined those states' political affairs. "If a community was self-supporting through and governed by its surrounding private landowners," noted classical historian Victor Davis Hanson writes, then they were the logical choice to fight that community's wars. The principal approach to a military threat was to "muster the largest, best-armed group of farmers to protect land in the quickest, cheapest, and most decisive way possible. It was far easier and more economical for farmers to defend farmland *on* farmland than to hire"[40] expensive and possibly untrustworthy foreigners to defend the state.

To support this specialized kind of militia-based warfare, average male Greek citizens learned how to fight at a young age. Moreover, almost all of them ended up fighting in a battle at least once in their lives, and more than a few became veterans of multiple conflicts. In their youth, their parents and peers repeatedly drilled into them a grim but certain reality. Namely, at any given moment in time their patriotism and bravery, along with that of their fellow citizen-soldiers, might be all that stood between their nation-state's survival and destruction. Indeed, in some cases defeat in a single battle could cause a city-state to collapse and its entire population to end up in slavery. Greeks everywhere were well aware of the example of Sparta's brutal conquest of Messenia and enslavement of its population.

Whatever Weapons They Could Afford

War—including fashioning weapons and armor, learning to use them, and training for and fighting battles—was an expected and frequent aspect of life in the city-states. These facts naturally caused Greek society to develop a complex set of traditions, customs, and rituals surrounding warfare. Some of those rituals appear strange or even absurd to people today.

A good example is the overly formal, honor-driven approach to bat-

A hoplight (center) prepares for battle. As a member of the Greek infantry, the hoplite wore a helmet and armor and carried a shield.

tle employed particularly when Greeks fought other Greeks. More often than not, there were no ambushes or other devious strategies. Instead, the two armies agreed to meet each other at a given time on an open, flat plain where large, strictly organized infantry formations called phalanxes met face-to-face. This kind of battle was in essence a "massed duel," in military historian F.E. Adcock's words, as well as "a trial of strength."[41]

The personal and societal preparations for such massed duels—including obtaining proper weapons and armor, training, and engaging in precombat rituals—were many and complicated. First, during the Classical Age local governments did not supply soldiers with uniforms and weapons, as is the case in modern armies. Rather, it was usually up to the citizen-soldiers themselves to obtain whatever armor and weapons they could afford. For example, wealthy men were the only citizens who had the means to own and train horses, which were very expensive. So when cavalry was used in battle (which was not often in this period), such units of mounted fighters were made up of well-to-do individuals.

The armor and weapons used by the hoplites, though not as costly as horses, were expensive enough that a man had to be at least middle-class to afford them. So most hoplites were middle or upper-middle class. Members of the poorer classes, who could not be hoplites or horsemen, most often served as support troops. They generally wore no armor and either wielded spears or slings in land battles or became oarsmen for the navy (if their city-state had one).

Training and Weapons

All fighters in an ancient Greek nation-state required some amount of training. But hoplites, who made up the heart of the land armies, needed and got the most extensive instruction in weapons use. Most often, a father who had served or still served as a hoplite began his son's training as soon as the child could hold wooden practice weapons.

In Athens, when a hoplite recruit turned eighteen, he continued that military schooling in a two-year course sponsored by the state. Called an *ephebe*, he was obliged to swear a patriotic oath that stated in part,

> WORDS IN CONTEXT
> *ephebe*
> A young Athenian man in training to become a hoplite.

"I will not shame the sacred arms, nor will I abandon my comrade wherever I am stationed. I will fight for the defense of the sacred rites both divine and human, and I shall not leave my country diminished when I die, but greater and more powerful, as far as I am able and with the help of all."[42]

In his first year of training, an *ephebe* drilled in weapons use and battlefield maneuvers. During the second year, he served his country by guarding its borders. Then, from ages twenty to sixty, he remained on call as a hoplite militiaman and was expected to defend the city-state if it was attacked.

The extensive array of armor and weapons an *ephebe* trained with and

Looking Back

The Noises of Human Misery

In these excerpts from his classic study of hoplite warfare, *The Western Way of War*, noted scholar Victor Davis Hanson provides a vivid description of the awful sounds of ancient Greek battle.

The entire noise of men and equipment was concentrated onto the small area of the ancient battlefield, itself usually a small plain encircled by mountains, which only improved the acoustics. . . . It was not just that the decibel level of Greek battle increased as the two phalanxes neared and met. The *nature* of the sound also changed from that of recognizable human speech—the war cry or song—and the reassuring jostling of equipment on the move to a terrible cacophony of smashed bronze, wood, and flesh. . . . The Greeks recognized that the peculiar noise of the initial crash came from a variety of sources. First, there was the dull thud of bronze against wood as either the metal spear point made its way through the wood core of a hoplite shield, or as soldiers struck their shields against the bronze breastplates and helmets of the enemy. [Meanwhile] the live sounds were more animal-like than human: the concerted groans of men exerting themselves, pushing forward in group effort with their bodies and shields against the immovable armor of the enemy.

Victor Davis Hanson, *The Western Way of War: Infantry Battle in Classical Greece.* Berkeley: University of California Press, 2009, pp. 152–53.

sometimes later employed in actual battle was called the panoply. Its most fundamental element was the shield, or *aspis*. Roughly 3 feet (1 m) across and weighing about 17 pounds (8 kg), it was composed of a wooden core often covered by layers of ox hide, a coating of bronze, or both. Another key feature of the panoply was the *cuirass*, or breastplate, which each hoplite wore to protect his torso. Several different types of cuirasses existed. But the most common was "made up of numerous layers of linen or canvas glued together to form a stiff shirt," military historian John Warry explains. It "wrapped around the body and was laced together on the left-hand side, where the join was protected by the shield. A yoke which bent down over the shoulders and tied to the chest completed the cuirass."[43] Another element of a hoplite's panoply was his bronze helmet, which was essential to protect his head from serious injury. He also donned bronze shin guards called greaves, which were sometimes molded to look like leg muscles.

WORDS IN CONTEXT

paean

A battle hymn sung by Greek soldiers before a battle.

To put one on, a soldier first pulled it open and then clipped it in place, in the same way that one applies a modern ear cuff. Also part of the panoply was the hoplite's main weapon, a 7-foot-long (2 m) thrusting spear. In addition to its iron tip, it featured a sharp butt spike in the rear, with which a fighter could defend himself if the spearhead broke off. His other backup weapon was a sword with an iron blade approximately 2 feet (61 cm) long, customarily used when his spear was lost or useless.

Into Battle

A hoplite's panoply was too heavy and burdensome to wear off the battlefield. So he got into his armor with the aid of a servant shortly before the fight began. The servant also took care of the mule that carried the panoply, along with the tent and supplies the two men required on the march. In Athens and presumably a number of other states, the government paid both the fighter and servant a small stipend for taking part in the military campaign.

When the opposing armies reached the place of battle and were ready to fight, the hoplites marched out and formed their phalanxes. Each consisted of a block of soldiers about eight ranks (lines) deep. (Commanders called for more or fewer than eight ranks if they felt it was warranted.) The length of a phalanx ranged from as little as a few hundred feet (or meters) to 1 mile (1.6 km) or more, depending on the number of fighters and the formation's depth. It was important to try to match or exceed the length of the enemy's line; otherwise, the opposing soldiers might outflank, or move around and behind, one's own formation.

When the opposing phalanxes had fully formed, they were a truly impressive sight. The men in each rank stood only about 3 feet (1 m) apart so that when they held up their shields they formed a massive, unbroken protective barrier. In front of these assembled fighters, the leading general sacrificed a goat or other animal to appease the city-state's patron deity. Then he usually delivered a short patriotic speech to raise everyone's spirits. If the two armies stood well apart and one's phalanx moved forward toward the enemy at a walk, the men might sing their national paean, or battle hymn. (In contrast, Spartan hoplites were accompanied by flutists, who played while marching straight at the enemy.)

Eventually, at the appropriate moment, one or the other general signaled his trumpeters to blast away, and the men of the phalanx charged forward at a run. They shouted their war cry as they went. Describing that dramatic moment in a battle in which he fought, Xenophon said, "We broke into a ringing cheer . . . and all charged at the double."[44]

As the opposing formations finally smashed into each other, the fighters in the front ranks began stabbing their spears at their opponents, looking for rare openings in the mouth, neck, and groin area. Meanwhile, the men in the rear ranks engaged in a maneuver known as the *othismos*. It literally translates as "the shoving." Using their shields, they pushed at the backs of their comrades in the front lines, pressing them forward toward the enemy. As Hanson says:

> **WORDS IN CONTEXT**
> *othismos*
> A Greek battle maneuver in which fighters in the rear ranks of a phalanx pushed at the backs of their companions in the front ranks, driving them forward.

Victorious Greek warriors erect a monument to their triumphant win. In typical fashion it consists of a framework that holds captured enemy weapons.

One indication of the tremendous force generated by this mass of shields was the nature of the casualties inflicted after the initial impact. There are many references [in Greek literature] to men who either were trampled down or literally suffocated as they stood. Any man who stumbled or fell wounded was in danger of being ground up as the men in the rear lumbered forward, blinded by dust and the press of bodies.[45]

When Greeks Fought Non-Greeks

At some point one of the phalanxes could no longer withstand the horrible pressure of the shoving and the massacre of men in the front ranks. That formation retreated and the battle was, for all intents and purposes, over. The losing soldiers returned to their homes, hoping to make a better showing in any future battles. Only rarely did the winning fighters pursue their opponents and try to destroy their homeland. Meanwhile, there on the field, the winning side erected a monument to commemorate its victory. Typically, it consisted of a wooden framework on which to hang captured enemy weapons.

The battle scene described here, including its fairly tame outcome, was typical only when Greeks fought Greeks. (Again, Sparta's conquest of Messenia was an exception to the rule.) Usually, however, the results of battles in which Greek hoplites fought non-Greeks were quite different. First, in the Classical era Greek hoplites were by far the best and most lethal fighters in the Mediterranean world. No foreign troops, including Persian ones, could stand up to a large Greek phalanx.

Indeed, ancient accounts frequently describe that formation striking abject fear into the enemy ranks. For example, a large battle between Persians and Greeks took place in Persia's heartland midway through the Classical Age. Xenophon, who was there, later wrote, "The two lines were hardly six or seven hundred yards apart when the Greeks began to chant the battle hymn and moved against the enemy." Soon the Greeks charged and "beat their spears on their shields to scare the [Persian] horses." Then suddenly, as the moving phalanx neared the enemy lines, the terrified Persians panicked and "turned and fled." Xenophon added that "not one Greek was hurt in this battle, except one on the left wing, said to have been shot by an arrow."[46]

Also, when outsiders directly attacked Greece—as the Persians did in 490 BCE and again ten years later, for instance—Greek hoplites tended to inflict massive slaughter and take few or no prisoners. This is what occurred after the Greeks won the battle of Plataea against an invading Persian army in 479 BCE. The enraged hoplites pursued the retreating enemy to their camp, smashed its defenses, and went on a merciless killing spree. Such displays of the Greeks' "lethal brand of

In Their Own Words

A Fatal Lack of Unity

Most ancient Greek citizen-soldiers were patriotic and coura-geous. But one crucial quality that most Greeks lacked was a spirit of unity. Their city-states and kingdoms endlessly fought one another, making them easy prey for the Romans, who swiftly conquered the Greek states. Well before that happened, a Greek orator, Agelaus of Aetolia, foresaw the coming danger. In 213 BCE, in the midst of war between Rome and Carthage, he warned his fellow Greeks that they needed to unite. "It would be best of all if the Greeks never went to war with one another," Agelaus said.

> If [only] they could regard it as the greatest gift of the gods for them all to speak with one voice, and could join hands like men who are crossing a river. In this way, they could unite to repulse the incursions of the barbar-ians and to preserve themselves and their cities. . . . We [Greeks] should consult one another and remain on our guard, in view of the huge armies which have been mo-bilized, and the vast scale of the war which is now being waged in the west. For it must already be obvious to all those who pay even the slightest attention to affairs of state that whether the Carthaginians defeat the Romans or the Romans the Carthaginians, the victors will by no means be satisfied with the sovereignty of Italy and Sicily, but will come here, and will advance both their forces and their ambitions beyond the bounds of justice.

Quoted in Polybius, *Histories*. Published as Polybius, *The Rise of the Roman Empire*, trans. Ian Scott-Kilvert. New York: Penguin, 1979, pp. 299–300.

warfare," Hanson points out, set a frightful standard and "have characterized the Western military tradition ever since."[47]

Rowers, Naval Backers, and Marines

The fight at Plataea and many of the other battles between Greeks and Persians took place on land. Yet Athens and several other Greek poleis also had navies in which hundreds and sometimes thousands of their citizens expressed their patriotism by defending their societies. A majority of those sailors were rowers, whose raw muscle power propelled their ships on ramming runs to destroy enemy vessels. There were also a few more skilled sailors who acted as crewmen, steering the ships and seeing to the masts and rigging.

During the Classical era naval battles were in a sense a modified form of hoplite warfare. There were no phalanxes aboard the ships, but the oarsmen and crew rarely engaged directly with the enemy. Instead, in a battle at least ten and sometimes up to forty trained hoplites served aboard each warship. It was they, at times aided by a few archers, who did the actual fighting. (Modern experts often refer to those infantrymen as "marines" to differentiate them from land-based hoplites.) This shows that one important naval tactic was to board an enemy ship and fight hand to hand, as in a land battle. The other principal tactic was to sink enemy ships by ramming them.

The Greek warships were mainly triremes. (The word *trireme* comes from a Greek term meaning "three oarsmen." It refers to the fact that the ship had three banks of rowers.) The Athenian state built them, and local well-to-do citizens maintained them (as part of the liturgy system), fulfilling their duty to give back to society on a yearly basis. Each trireme was roughly 130 feet (40 m) long and 18 feet (5.5 m) wide. Of a total crew of around 200 men, 170 of them manned the oars; 15 were deckhands who ran the ship; One was the captain, who had general charge of the ship; and one played a flute to keep time for the rowers. The rest were hoplites and archers.

Adding in the carpenters and other skilled craftsmen who actually built such a vessel, it clearly required a lot of local citizens to send a single

During a battle at sea, a Greek warship sinks one enemy ship and pursues another. The Greeks favored tactics such as boarding enemy ships and engaging in hand-to-hand combat or ramming and sinking the ships.

warship into battle. From that it follows that only a few rich city-states with hefty populations could afford to maintain formidable navies. It is not surprising, therefore, that Athens—the wealthiest and most populous state in the Classical Age—had by far the biggest and strongest navy. In about 420 BCE it boasted at least 350 warships, then viewed as an enormous naval force.

One important factor that limited the effectiveness of triremes in wartime was that they were not practical for long-term naval strategy. This was because they were fairly narrow and shallow, and most of their interior space was taken up by the rowers and their benches and oars. As a result, they lacked eating and sleeping facilities. In turn, that meant they were unable to stay at sea for long periods and had to be beached at least once a day. Xenophon described an Athenian admiral whose men were ready for their evening meal. "He would order the leading ships" of his fleet to turn toward "the land, and at a signal make them race to the shore. And it was something really to be proud of to be the first to get water or whatever else was wanted and to be the first to get one's meal."[48]

To Kill or Be Killed

Although the two chief battle tactics of these warships were ramming an enemy vessel and getting close enough to allow one's marines to board the enemy and fight hand-to-hand, the Greeks had a third common maneuver. This involved attacking an opposing ship at an angle and shearing off several of its oars. That left the hull more open to both ramming and boarding.

All of these tactics were employed to great effect in one of the most decisive naval battles of ancient times. During the huge Persian invasion of Greece in 480 BCE, a united Greek navy led by Athens met the much larger Persian fleet in the bay of Salamis, a few miles from Athens's urban center. Fighting for their homes and way of life (and unbeknownst to them, the very future of Western civilization), the Greek sailors and hoplites achieved a stunning victory.

The Athenian playwright Aeschylus, who fought on one of those triremes that day, later wrote, "A Greek ship charged first, and chopped off the whole stern of a Persian galley. Then charge followed charge on every side." Also, savage hand-to-hand fighting raged all across the bay. "The Greeks seized fragments of wrecks and broken oars," Aeschylus continued, "and hacked and stabbed" and soon "the sea was hidden, carpeted with wrecks and dead men."[49]

The idea that butchery of this sort was inevitable now and then to keep one's homeland safe from the threat of utter destruction became a simple fact of life for most Greeks. A clear majority of a polis's men knew what it was like to kill or be killed by spears and swords at close quarters. Moreover, they fought knowing that if they lost, their families and friends back home might be next to die. That their entire society and way of life might hang in the balance was a constant reality of living in the Greek lands.

Source Notes

Introduction: An Extraordinary Legacy

1. C.M. Bowra, *Classical Greece*. New York: Time-Life, 1977, pp. 11–12.

Chapter One: Houses and Their Contents

2. Alfred Zimmern, *The Greek Commonwealth: Politics and Economics in Fifth-Century Athens*. Charleston, SC: Nabu, 2013, pp. 66–67.
3. Demosthenes, *On Organization*, in *Demosthenes: Olynthiacs, Philippics, Minor Speeches*, trans. J.H. Vince. Cambridge, MA: Harvard University Press, 1985, pp. 371, 373.
4. R.E. Wycherley, *How the Greeks Built Cities*. New York: Norton, 1962, pp. 175–77.
5. Quoted in Plutarch, "Life of Demosthenes," in "Plutarch," *The Age of Alexander: Nine Greek Lives*, trans. Ian Scott-Kilvert. New York: Penguin, 1973, pp. 197–98.
6. Andrew Dalby, *Siren Feasts: A History of Food and Gastronomy in Greece*. New York: Routledge, 1996, p. 23.
7. Joint Associations of Classical Teachers, *The World of Athens*. New York: Cambridge University Press, 1984, p. 127.

Chapter Two: Family Members, Roles, and Duties

8. Plato, "Statesman," in *The Dialogues of Plato*, Robert Maynard Hutchins, ed., trans. Benjamin Jowett. Chicago: Britannica, 1952, p. 581.
9. Xenophon, *Oeconomicus*, in Xenophon, *Memorabilia and Oeconomicus*, trans. E.C. Marchant. Cambridge, MA: Harvard University Press, 1965, p. 415.
10. Xenophon, *Oeconomicus*, pp. 429, 423.
11. Sarah B. Pomeroy, *Goddesses, Whores, Wives, and Slaves: Women in Classical Antiquity*. New York: Schocken, 1995, p. 63.
12. Robert Flaceliere, *Daily Life in Greece at the Time of Pericles*, trans. Peter Green. London: Phoenix, 1996, pp. 62–63.

13. Flaceliere, *Daily Life in Greece at the Time of Pericles*, pp. 63–64.

14. Helen Schrader, "Sparta Reconsidered: Marriage," Elysium Gates, September 2012. http://elysiumgates.com.

15. Plutarch, *Life of Lycurgus*, in *Plutarch on Sparta*, trans. Richard J.A. Talbert. New York: Penguin, 1988, pp. 25–26.

16. Zimmern, *The Greek Commonwealth*, p. 74.

17. Plato, *Laws*, in *The Dialogues of Plato*, p. 723.

18. Antiphon, *On the Murder of Herodes*, in Kathleen Freeman, *The Murder of Herodes and Other Trials from the Athenian Law Courts*. New York: Norton, 1963, p. 74.

Chapter Three: Community Life and Religion

19. Quoted in Plutarch, *Life of Solon*, in "Plutarch," *The Rise and Fall of Athens: Nine Greek Lives*, trans. Ian Scott-Kilvert. New York: Penguin, 1983, p. 60.

20. Michael Grant, *The Rise of the Greeks*. New York: Macmillan, 2001, p. 69.

21. John Camp and Elizabeth Fisher, *The World of the Ancient Greeks*. London: Thames & Hudson, 2002, pp. 122–23.

22. Demosthenes, *On the Crown*, in *The Classical Greek Reader*, ed. Kenneth J. Atchity. New York: Oxford University Press, 1998, pp. 218–19.

23. Quoted in Xenophon, *Hellenica*. Published as Xenophon, *A History of My Times*, George Cawkwell, trans. Rex Warner. New York: Penguin, 1979, p. 127.

24. Pindar, *Nemean Odes*, in *The Odes of Pindar*, trans. C.M. Bowra. New York: Penguin, 1985, p. 206.

25. John Boardman, *The Parthenon and Its Sculptures*. Austin: University of Texas Press, 1985, p. 19.

26. Plato, *Laws*, in *The Dialogues of Plato*, p. 788.

27. Quoted in Xenophon, "Memorabilia," in Xenophon, *Conversations of Socrates*, trans. Hugh Tredennick and Robin Waterfield. New York: Penguin, 1990, p. 93.

Chapter Four: Sports and Other Leisure Activities

28. Edith Hamilton, *The Greek Way*. New York: Norton, 1993, pp. 24–25.

29. Pindar, *Nemean Odes*, p. 236.

30. Plato, *Symposium*, trans. Tom Griffith. Berkeley: University of California Press, 1985, sect. 176a.

31. Flaceliere, *Daily Life in Greece at the Time of Pericles*, p. 181.

32. Xenophon, "Symposium," in Xenophon, *Conversations of Socrates*, pp. 230–31.

33. Pindar, *Nemean Odes*, p. 29.

34. Aristotle, *Poetics*, in *Introduction to Aristotle*, ed. Richard McKeon. New York: Random House, 1947, p. 629.

35. Victor Ehrenberg, *The People of Aristophanes: A Sociology of Old Attic Comedy*. New York: Schocken, 1962, p. 26.

36. Galen, *Exercise with the Small Ball*, in *Galen: Selected Works*, trans. P.N. Singer. New York: Oxford University Press, 1997, pp. 299–300.

37. Waldo E. Sweet, ed., *Sport and Recreation in Ancient Greece: A Sourcebook with Translations*. New York: Oxford University Press, 1987, p. 155.

38. Quoted in Sweet, *Sport and Recreation in Ancient Greece*, p. 158.

39. Hamilton, *The Greek Way*, p. 25.

Chapter Five: Patriotism, Warfare, and Survival

40. Victor Davis Hanson, *The Wars of the Ancient Greeks and Their Invention of Western Military Culture*. London: Cassell, 2000, p. 50.

41. F.E. Adcock, *The Greek and Macedonian Art of War*. Berkeley: University of California Press, 1962, p. 7.

42. Quoted in N.R.E. Fisher, *Social Values in Classical Athens*. London: Dent, 1976, pp. 152–53.

43. John Warry, *Warfare in the Classical World*. Norman: University of Oklahoma Press, 2001, p. 35.

44. Xenophon, *Anabasis*, trans. W.H.D. Rouse. New York: New American Library, 1959, p. 38.

45. Victor Davis Hanson, *The Western Way of War: Infantry Battle in Classical Greece*. Berkeley: University of California Press, 2009, p. 175.

46. Xenophon, *Anabasis*, p. 38.

47. Hanson, *The Wars of the Ancient Greeks and Their Invention of Western Military Culture*, pp. 19–20.

48. Xenophon, *Hellenica*, p. 313.

49. Aeschylus, *The Persians*, in Aeschylus, *Prometheus Bound and Other Plays, The Suppliants, Seven Against Thebes, The Persians*, trans. Philip Vellacott. Baltimore: Penguin, 1961, p. 134.

For Further Research

Books

Alastair Blanshard and Kim Shahabudin, *Classics on Screen: Ancient Greece and Rome on Film*. New York: Bloomsbury, 2011.

Paul Cartledge, *Ancient Greece: A Very Short Introduction*. New York: Oxford University Press, 2011.

Charles Freeman, *Egypt, Greece, and Rome: Civilizations of the Ancient Mediterranean*. New York: Oxford University Press, 2014.

Robert Garland, *Ancient Greece: Everyday Life in the Birthplace of Western Civilization*. New York: Sterling, 2013.

Victor Davis Hanson, *The Western Way of War: Infantry Battle in Classical Greece*. Berkeley: University of California Press, 2009.

Amie Leavitt, *Ancient Athens*. Hockessin, DE: Mitchell Lane, 2012.

Fiona MacDonald, *I Wonder Why the Greeks Built Temples*. New York: Kingfisher, 2012.

Bonnie MacLachlan, *Women in Ancient Greece: A Sourcebook*. New York: Bloomsbury Academic, 2012.

Thomas R. Martin, *Ancient Greece: From Prehistoric to Hellenistic Times*. New Haven, CT: Yale University Press, 2013.

Don Nardo, *Ancient Greek Art and Architecture*. Farmington Hills, MI: Gale/Cengage, 2012.

Anne Pearson, *Ancient Greece*. London: Dorling Kindersley, 2014.

Sarah B. Pomeroy et al. *Ancient Greece: A Political, Social, and Cultural History*. New York: Oxford University Press, 2011.

Nigel Rodgers, *The Illustrated Encyclopedia of Ancient Greece*. London: Lorenz, 2012.

Charlie Samuels, *Technology in Ancient Greece*. New York: Gareth Stevens, 2011.

Websites

Ancient Greece (http://richard-hooker.com/sites/worldcultures/GREECE/GREECE.HTM). Noted scholar Richard Hooker discusses the origins of ancient Greek drama and the types of plays presented in Greek theaters.

Ancient Olympics, Perseus Digital Library (www.perseus.tufts.edu /Olympics). The Perseus Digital Library is the largest and most reliable single online source for ancient Greek history and culture. Its section on the ancient Olympics contains a wealth of useful information.

Democratic Experiment, BBC (www.bbc.co.uk/history/ancient/greeks /greekdemocracy_01.shtml). World-class classical historian Paul Cartledge delves into the democratic institutions of ancient Athens and their influence on other Greek states.

Everyday Life in Ancient Greece, EyeWitness to History.com (www .eyewitnesstohistory.com/ancientgreece.htm). Using primary source quotes, this excellent site looks at the lives of members of Greek society's upper classes.

Greek Gods and Religious Practices, Metropolitan Museum of Art (www.metmuseum.org/toah/hd/grlg/hd_grlg.htm). One of the world's greatest museums offers this easy-to-read overview of Greek religious practices. For a lot more information on the subject, see the sources listed in the article's bibliography.

Greeks: Crucible of Civilization, PBS (www.pbs.org/empires/the greeks). This overview of ancient Greek history and culture is an excellent introduction to the Greeks.

History of Greek Literature, History World (www.historyworld.net /wrldhis/PlainTextHistories.asp?historyid=aa17). Respected scholar, writer, and television personality Bamber Gascoigne wrote this fulsome, accurate introduction to Greek literature, including works by Homer, Herodotus, Plato, Aristophanes, Thucydides, Xenophon, and several others.

Women in the Ancient World (www.womenintheancientworld.com). James C. Thompson, a noted researcher and scholar of ancient Greek life, concisely describes the duties and living conditions of women in the ancient world, including Greek women.

Index

Note: Boldface page numbers indicate illustrations.

Picture Credits

Cover: © National Geographic Society/Corbis

Maury Aaseng: 16

© Stefano Bianchetti/Corbis: 21, 30, 51, 76, 80

© Heritage Images/Corbis: 58

© National Geographic Society/Corbis: 26, 44, 49

© Tarker/Corbis: 71

Thinkstock Images: 8–9

Greek Theatre, Jackson, Peter (1922–2003)/Private Collection/© Look and Learn/Bridgeman Images: 12

Writing lesson in ancient Athens, Payne, Roger (b.1934)/Private Collection/© Look and Learn/Bridgeman Images: 36

A Spartan whipping his slaves (gouache on paper), Jackson, Peter (1922–2003)/Private Collection/© Look and Learn/Bridgeman Images: 38

Ancient Athens—reconstruction of the Symposium (colour litho), Italian School/Private Collection/De Agostini Picture Library/Bridgeman Images: 62

Relief depicting Menander with theatrical masks, copy of a Greek original (marble), Roman/Museo Gregoriano Profano, Vatican Museums, Vatican City/Alinari/Bridgeman Images: 65

About the Author

Historian and award-winning author Don Nardo has written numerous books about the ancient world, its peoples, and their cultures, including volumes on the Babylonians, Assyrians, Persians, Minoans, Greeks, Etruscans, Romans, Carthaginians, and others. He is also the author of single-volume encyclopedias on ancient Mesopotamia, ancient Greece, ancient Rome, and Greek and Roman mythology. Nardo, who also composes and arranges orchestral music, lives with his wife, Christine, in Massachusetts.